Sirtfood Diet Recipes

A Cookbook Meal Plan Guide to Lose Weight, Eat Healthier, and Burn Fat by Activating Your Skinny Gene with Secret Recipes for a Healthy Diet Plan and Tasty Preparations

Aidan Life

COPYRIGHT

TABLE OF CONTENTS

INTRODUCTION

Celeb gets more fit. Celeb gets captured appearing to be unique. Fans go wild and are *dying* to know precisely how they did it. Enter: Adele! The artist was spotted a year ago (and again on an ongoing excursion in Anguilla) with an observably slimmer figure, and individuals are very inquisitive about the eating plan she allegedly follows: the Sirtfood Diet.

While Adele hasn't spoken openly about her weight reduction, the New York Post asserted that she has shed 50 pounds by following the eating plan (and her name was initially appended to the eating routine in 2016). A previous mentor of the star additionally as of late revealed to The Sun that she accepts the adjustments in Adele's body boil down to "90 percent diet."

The Sirtfood Diet has purportedly gotten love from various celebs notwithstanding the "Somebody Like You" artist, including Pippa Middleton and renowned competitors like previous ace fighter David Haye.

The short form: The Sirtfood Diet is said to be wealthy in nourishments that contain a specific supplement that helps trigger qualities in the body associated with fat misfortune and fat stockpiling (more on this in a moment). What's more, a few people say they love it in light of the fact that there are some entirely scrumptious nourishments that have these unique supplements (greetings, wine and chocolate), so you don't feel denied.

But...is the Sirtfood Diet unrealistic? Here's all that you have to think about the goodness so-buzzy-right-now weight reduction strategy, with contribution from nourishment specialists Caroline Apovian, MD, chief of the Nutrition and Weight Management Center at the Boston Medical Center, and Edwina Clark, RD, head of sustenance and wellbeing for Yummly.

To begin with, what is the Sirtfood Diet precisely?

The eating regimen originates from the book of a similar name. The creators—Aidan Goggins and Glen Matten—of The Sirtfood Diet exhort eating for the most part nourishments rich in sirtuins, a sort of protein in plant nourishments. "The eating plan itself is intended to 'turn on' the sirtuin qualities (especially SIRT-1), which are accepted to support digestion, increment fat consuming, battle aggravation, and control craving," says Clark.

Early investigations propose that calorie limitation and resveratrol (a polyphenol found in nourishments like grapes, blueberries, and peanuts), initiate the SIRT-1 quality, and these two standards support the Sirtfood way to deal with eating.

What does the arrangement involve?

The eating regimen keeps going a sum of three weeks and is separated into two stages.

Stage one: You constrain yourself to three Sirtfood green juices (containing kale, arugula, parsley, celery, green apple, lemon squeeze, and green tea) and one Sirtfood-rich supper every day, totaling around 1,000 calories every day, says Dr. Apovian, MD. For the following four days, you drink two Sirtfood green squeezes and eat two Sirtfood-rich dinners, which brings your calorie aggregate to around 1,500 every day.

Stage two: This is the upkeep organize, which keeps going 14 days. During those two weeks, you should have three Sirtfood-rich dinners and one Sirtfood green squeeze day by day.

When those three weeks are up, there's no set intend to follow. To proceed on the Sirtfood way, you should simply change every one of your suppers to incorporate whatever number Sirtfoods as could be allowed. Exercise is likewise supported (30 minutes of movement, five days per week), however getting sweat-soaked isn't the primary focal point of the weight reduction plan.

What are "sirtfoods"?

Sirtfoods are any nourishment that is rich is the sirtuin protein, which is sort of plant-based protein that has given some guarantee in clinical examinations to improve metabolic wellbeing. Sirtfoods include:

Medjool dates

Blueberries

Espresso

Kale

Arugula

Parsley

Celery

Green apple

Soy

Strawberries

85 percent cocoa chocolate

Turmeric

You can get a total rundown of sirtfoods prescribed on the eating regimen inside the book.

ooo, would you be able to get more fit on the eating regimen?

The Sirtfood Diet incorporates numerous nutritious nourishments that are gainful for weight reduction, for example, celery, kale, green tea, Medjool dates, lean chicken, lean red meat, and parsley, says Dr. Apovian. The eating regimen likewise confines or takes out numerous nourishments that are known to cause weight increase, for example, refined flours, included sugars, and prepared food sources with practically no dietary benefit. Furthermore, because of that strangely low calorie admission, devotees will probably get more fit gave they stay on course, she says.

"Proof to date proposes that caloric limitation and discontinuous fasting can be a viable technique for weight reduction and improving metabolic wellbeing," says Clark. "In any case, this may not be proper for everybody," she says.

Are there any drawbacks?

The long haul manageability of this arrangement is faulty. When you're past the initial scarcely any weeks, there's no eating technique to follow other than adding more Sirtfoods to every feast. This makes the eating routine substantially more adaptable than most, which is an enormous advantage, yet a three-week significant lot of hardship could without much of a stretch lead to gorging during stage two, at last setting you back at the starting point.

Regardless of whether you're uber-trained, this is as yet an extreme eating regimen to follow. "A minor 1,000 calories will leave a great many people feeling exceptionally ravenous," says Dr. Apovian. Also, in case you're not an aficionado of green squeeze, a staple of the primary week, that will make you much hungrier, she says. Additionally, since the vast majority of the weight reduction in stage one is water weight, it will return directly on once you continue ordinary eating, she says.

Also, following any eating regimen that does exclude a solid measure of protein (e.g., during the principal seven day stretch of the Sirtfood Diet), may bring about muscle misfortune and a more slow digestion, says Dr. Apovian. To shed pounds and keep it off, building muscle through eating a lot of protein and working out with loads is fundamental.

Over all that, examine on SIRT-1 initiating nourishments is still especially in its outset, so it's vague in the case of expending polyphenol-rich nourishments substantially affects weight in everybody. "Weight is a multi-faceted idea, including complex associations between our one of a kind hereditary cosmetic and our eating regimen, development designs, rest propensities, and passionate state," notes Clark.

At last, eating an eating regimen wealthy in an assortment of solid nourishments, including lean protein sources, various leafy foods, and entire grains is a more advantageous, progressively manageable approach to get more fit and keep it off, says Dr. Apovian.

HOW TO FOLLOW THE SIRTFOOD DIET

In the realm of diet and nourishment, there's constantly another approach to shed pounds.

The most recent technique, upheld by any semblance of Pippa Middleton and Adele, was laid out in detail not long ago in a book called the SirtFood Diet, which gives a sustenance plan based on nourishments like kale, green tea, dim chocolate, wine, blueberries, olive oil, soy, and different food sources high in specific plant exacerbates that invigorate proteins called sirtuins.

"Sirtuins are a class of proteins found in living things"— including people—"that exploration has demonstrated to be engaged with significant organic procedures, for example, maturing, cell demise, aggravation, and digestion," says Stacy Sims, Ph.D., a games nourishment master and senior research individual at the Adams Center for High Performance at the University of Waikato in New Zealand.

As such, sirtuins may assist you with living longer, and according to their advocates, they may likewise assist you with shedding muscle versus fat. The expectation is that eating a huge amount of sirtfoods will invigorate the sirtuin qualities (at times called thin qualities) along these lines to fasting. Yet, does it truly work that way? To begin with, some foundation: In well evolved creatures, there are seven kinds of sirtuins, which extend from SIRT1 to SIRT7. Of them, SIRT1 is the one that analysts are generally keen on, says Sims. "SIRT1 is some of the time alluded to as the 'gatekeeper' against oxidative pressure and DNA harm."

The possibility of the Sirtfood Diet is if you can actuate SIRT1, you can create more mitochondria, the powerhouse of the cells, which will help diminish oxidative pressure, permitting you to age more slow, says Mike Roussell, Ph.D., a dietary advisor in Philadelphia.

The issue? "You can't in any way, shape or form devour enough of the nourishments prescribed by this diet to increment sirtuins," says Roussell. Take red wine, which is remembered for the SirtFood Diet: "To get 20 milligrams of resveratrol [an cancer prevention agent that invigorates SIRT1], you would need to drink in excess of 40 glasses of wine," Roussell says. Which, all things considered, we aren't proposing you do.

Additionally, inquire about from Endocrine Journal finds that SIRT1 directs craving differently from individual to individual. "So for certain individuals, expanded SIRT1 articulation may make you hungry," says Roussell.

Presently, the way that individuals get more fit by following the SirtFood Diet likely boils down to two elements:

The nourishments in the arrangement will in general be wealthy in supplements.

The book requires seven days of exceptional calorie limitation—only 1,000 calories every day for the initial three days and 1,500 per day for the remainder of the week. Furthermore, the vast majority of those calories are from juice.

Confining calories, as you presumably know, is the most dependable system for getting in shape. What's more, for what it's worth, inquire about from Finland's Helsinki University found that low-calorie diets may normally increment sirtuin action, whether or not you're eating sirtuin-rich nourishments or not.

So sure, add a couple sirtuin nourishments to your diet: kale, strawberries, pecans, buckwheat, celery, red onions—all great stuff. Be that as it may, don't expect that you can't eat whatever else. If you're not kidding about getting thinner, center around lean protein, vegetables, and entire grains—and hold your all out vitality admission down.

You can decide your optimal weight-loss calorie objective by finding your resting metabolic rate (the number cruncher at My Fitness Pal can help) and afterward duplicating it by 1.3, says Krista Austin, Ph.D., an activity physiology and sports sustenance master. Go any lower than that, and you chance easing back your digestion down.

"As wellbeing crazes go, there's almost no to state against sirtfoods," closes Sims. "Notwithstanding, these are basically one feature of a sound diet. Nobody needs to purchase a sirtfood cookbook."

As we head into 2020, setting out on another health plan is no uncertainty at the highest point of your schedule. If you've attempted and bombed a diet plan, Dry January or veganuary, the SIRT wellbeing plan could be the perfect choice for a more joyful, more advantageous you. Right off the bat, it incorporates chocolate and red wine so we're promptly intrigued. Peruse on to find all that you have to think about the SIRT diet...

What's going on here?

The Sirtfood diet plan sounds unrealistic as it permits you to eat chocolate and drink red wine. Aidan Goggins and Glen Matten, the sustenance specialists behind the diet, guarantee that by eating nourishments wealthy in a sort of protein called sirtuin activators -

known as Sirtfoods - you can 'switch on your muscle to fat ratio's consuming forces'.

Medical advantages of tailing it:

Just as helping you feel invigorated, the sirtuin activators can help direct your digestion, increment muscle and consume fat, according to Goggins and Matten.

Symptoms:

The writers guarantee that the objective of the Sirt diet is more about good dieting than sensational weight loss, yet a few nutritionists have protested the way that their book is embellished with the slogan "lose 7lbs in 7 days". A loss of 1 to 2lbs seven days is viewed as a relentless and solid sum. So such sensational weight loss in a brief period may not be useful for your prosperity. Additionally, self-evident, however important: red wine is loaded with poisons, regardless of whether it is high in sirtuin activators, so swallowing it as a feature of a 'diet' presumably is definitely not a smart thought. Darn.

According to the book's slogan, there is potential for fast transient weight loss. This depends on an exacting arrangement, including calorie control - 1000 the initial three days, then increasing this to 1500 - and expending a set quantities of green juices and Sirtfood-rich suppers. In any case, in the long haul the objective is essentially to eat whatever number Sirtfoods as could be allowed.

Nourishments you ought to eat:

Red wine, dull chocolate (yes you read it right), green tea, escapades, citrus natural products, yet in addition apples and blueberries. Parsley, turmeric, kale are incredible green sirtfoods.

It's the most recent diet fever everybody's discussing, a diet rich in 'sirtfoods'. According to scientists, these unique nourishments work by enacting specific proteins in the body called sirtuins. Sirtuins are accepted to shield cells in the body from biting the dust when they are under pressure and are thought to manage aggravation, digestion and the maturing procedure. Analysts additionally accept sirtuins impact the body's capacity to consume fat and lift digestion, bringing about a seven pound weight loss seven days while looking after muscle.

The diet

So what are these mystical 'sirtfoods'? The ten most basic include:

Green Tea

Dull chocolate (that is at any rate 85 percent cocoa)

Apples

Citrus natural products

Parsley

Turmeric

Kale

Blueberries

Tricks

Red wine

The diet is a two stage approach; the underlying stage keeps going multi week and includes confining calories to 1000kcal for three days expending three sirtfood green juices and one dinner daily that is rich in sirtfoods. The juices incorporate kale, celery, rocket, parsley, green tea and lemon and suppers incorporate turkey escalope with sage, escapades and parsley, chicken and kale curry and prawn pan sear with buckwheat noodles. From days four to seven, admissions are expanded to 1500kcal involving two sirtfood green juices and two sirtfood-rich dinners daily.

The subsequent stage is known as the upkeep stage which keeps going 14 days where relentless weight loss happens. The creators trust it's a feasible and sensible approach to get in shape. In any case, concentrating on weight loss isn't what the diet is about – it's intended to be tied in with eating the best nourishments nature brings to the table. Long haul they suggest eating three adjusted sirtfood rich dinners daily alongside one sirtfood green juice.

A lady remaining on gauging scales in a washroom

Dietitian Emer Delaney says:

"From the start, this isn't a diet I would exhort for my customers. Planning to have 1000kcal for three back to back days is amazingly difficult and I accept most of individuals would be not able to accomplish it. Taking a gander at the rundown of nourishments, you can see they are the kind of things that often show up on a 'solid nourishment list', anyway it is smarter to empower these as a component of a sound adjusted diet. Having a glass of red wine or a modest quantity of chocolate periodically won't do us any damage - I wouldn't prescribe them every day. We ought to likewise be eating a blend of different foods grown from the ground and not only those on the rundown.

"Regarding weight loss and boosting digestion, individuals may have encountered a seven pound weight loss on the scales, however as far as I can tell this will be liquid. Consuming and losing fat requires some investment so it is incredibly impossible this weight loss is a loss of fat. I would be extremely careful of any diet that prescribes quick and unexpected weight loss as this just isn't attainable and will more than likely be a loss of liquid. When individuals come back to their standard dietary patterns, they will recapture the weight. Gradual weight loss is the key and for this we have to limit calories and increment our action levels. Gobbling adjusted normal suppers made up of low GI nourishments, lean protein, leafy foods and keeping very much hydrated is the most secure approach to get thinner."

If you're looking for another popular weight loss plan, you may have caught wind of the Sirtfood diet. Makers of the diet guarantee it encourages you shed pounds rapidly by enacting the equivalent "thin quality" pathways instigated by fasting and standard exercise. Find out about the Sirtfood diet will assist you with deciding whether attempting it is extremely worth your time and energy.

What is the Sirtfood Diet?

Makers of the Sirtfood diet say that nourishments rich in polyphenols (cancer prevention agents) turn on "thin" qualities in your body that copy exercise and fasting, kick off weight loss, support digestion, increment state of mind and improve maturing. Instances of polyphenol-rich nourishments the Sirtfood diet urges you to eat incorporate green tea, dull chocolate, espresso, red wine, and kale.

Sirtfood Meal Plans

When you follow the Sirtfood diet, you'll start with stage 1—which goes on for seven days. During the initial three days of the diet, you'll drink three Sirtfood squeezes and have one Sirtfood-rich dinner for a day by day aggregate of 1,000 calories. On days four however through seven you'll devour 1,500 complete calories, drink two green squeezes and eat two solid Sirtfood-rich suppers. This finishes stage 1.

Stage 2 endures 14 days and permits you to eat three adjusted Sirtfood-rich dinners and one green squeeze every day. After stage 2 is finished, you'll follow a progressively ordinary method for eating—however are urged to fuse sirtuin-actuating nourishments into normal supper plans. You can return stage 1 and 2 whenever you have to lose more weight or muscle to fat ratio.

Nourishments You Can Eat

You'll most likely need to buy a juicer when following the Sirtfood diet. The accompanying nourishments and beverages are supported:

Green juices (containing matcha green tea, lovage and buckwheat)

Green tea

Espresso

Cocoa powder

Dull chocolate

Turmeric

Kale

Onions

Parsley

Ginger

Olive oil

Red chicory

Soy yogurt

Natural products

Vegetables

Pecans

Eggs

Bacon

Turkey

Fish

Entire grain pitas

Cheddar

Hummus

Buckwheat noodles

Red wine

Avoid dairy nourishments when following the Sirtfood diet.

Does the Diet Work?

Scientists analyzed impacts of Sirtfoods (sirtuin-enacting nourishments) on wellbeing and weight the board. One 2013 investigation found that diets rich in Sirtfoods seem to help with sound maturing and constant ailment avoidance. A 2017 audit presumed that polyphenols seem to assist lower with bodying weight, blood glucose, and circulatory strain—however more research is required around there.

One explanation you'll likely shed pounds if you follow the Sirtfood diet accurately is on the grounds that you'll decrease calories (at any rate in stage 1) to 1,000 to 1,500 calories for each day, which is a nearly surefire approach to drop weight.

The primary concern is while you don't need to eat sirtuin-actuating nourishments to shed pounds (just bringing down your general calorie admission ought to work), most of Sirtfoods are sound, seem to bring down ailment dangers, and help in solid weight the board.

UNDERSTANDING SIRTUINS

Sirtuins help control your cell wellbeing. This is what you have to think about how they work, what they can accomplish for your body, and why they depend on NAD+ to work.

Sirtuins are a group of proteins that manage cell wellbeing. Sirtuins assume a key job in managing cell homeostasis. Homeostasis includes keeping the cell in balance. Be that as it may, sirtuins can just capacity within the sight of NAD+, nicotinamide adenine dinucleotide, a coenzyme found in every single living cell.

How Sirtuins Regulate Cellular Health with NAD+

Think about your body's cells like an office. In the workplace, there are numerous individuals working on different undertakings with an extreme objective: remain gainful and satisfy the strategic the organization in a proficient way for whatever length of time that conceivable. In the cells, there are numerous pieces working on different undertakings with an extreme objective, as well: remain solid and capacity proficiently for whatever length of time that conceivable. Similarly as needs in the organization change, because of different inner and outside components, so do needs in the cells. Somebody needs to run the workplace, controlling what completes when, who will do it and when to switch course. In the workplace, that would be your CEO. In the body, at the cell level, it's your sirtuins.

Sirtuins are a group of seven proteins that assume a job in cell wellbeing. Sirtuins can just capacity within the sight of NAD+, nicotinamide adenine dinucleotide, a coenzyme found in every single living cell. NAD+ is imperative to cell digestion and several other organic procedures. If sirtuins are an organization's CEO, then NAD+ is the cash that pays the compensation of the CEO and representatives, all while keeping the lights on and the workplace space lease paid. An organization, and the body, can't work without it. Yet, levels of NAD+ decrease with age, constraining the capacity of sirtuins with age too. Like everything in the human body, it isn't so basic. Sirtuins oversee everything that occurs in your cells.

Sirtuins Are Proteins. I'm not catching That's meaning?

Sirtuins are a group of proteins. Protein may seem like dietary protein — what's found in beans and meats and well, protein shakes — yet for this situation we're discussing particles called proteins, which work all through the body's phones in various different capacities. Consider proteins the divisions at an organization, every one concentrating without anyone else specific capacity while planning with different offices.

An outstanding protein in the body is hemoglobin, which is a piece of the globin group of proteins and is liable for shipping oxygen all through your blood. The myoglobin is the hemoglobin's partner, and together they make up the globin family.

Your body has almost 60,000 groups of proteins — a great deal of offices! — and sirtuins are one of those families. While hemoglobin is one out of a group of two proteins, sirtuins are a group of seven.

Of the seven sirtuins in the cell, three of them work in the mitochondria, three of them work in the core and one of them works in the cytoplasm, each assuming an assortment of jobs. The fundamental job of sirtuins, notwithstanding, is that they expel acetyl bunches from different proteins.

Acetyl bunches control specific responses. They're physical labels on proteins that different proteins perceive will respond with them. If proteins are the branches of the cell and DNA is the CEO, the acetyl bunches are the accessibility status of every division head. For instance, if a protein is accessible then the sirtuin can work with it to get something going, similarly as the CEO can work with an accessible division head to get something going.

Sirtuins work with acetyl bunches by doing what's called deacetylation. This implies they perceive there's an acetyl bunch on a particle then evacuate the acetyl gathering, which tees up the atom for its activity. One way that sirtuins work is by expelling acetyl gatherings (deacetylating) natural proteins, for example, histones. For instance, sirtuins deacetylate histones, proteins that are a piece of a dense type of DNA called chromatin. The histone is an enormous cumbersome protein that the DNA folds itself over. Consider it a Christmas tree, and the DNA strand is the strand of lights. When the histones have an acetyl gathering, the chromatin is open, or loosened up.

This loosened up chromatin implies the DNA is being interpreted, a basic procedure. Yet, it doesn't have to remain loosened up, as it's defenseless against harm in this position, practically like the Christmas lights could get tangled or the bulbs can get harmed when they're awkward or up for a really long time. When the histones are deacetylated by sirtuins, the chromatin is shut, or firmly and perfectly twisted, which means quality articulation is halted, or quieted.

We've just thought about sirtuins for around 20 years, and their essential capacity was found during the 1990s. From that point forward, specialists have rushed to examine them, identifying their significance while likewise bringing up issues about what else we can find out about them.

The Discovery and History of Sirtuins

Geneticist Dr. Amar Klar found the first sirtuin, called SIR2, during the 1970s, identifying it as a quality that controlled the capacity of yeast cells to mate. A long time later, during the 1990s, scientists found different qualities that were homologous — comparable in structure — to SIR2 in different living beings like worms, natural product flies, and these SIR2 homologues were then named sirtuins. There were different quantities of sirtuins in every creature. For instance, yeast has five sirtuins, microscopic organisms has one, mice have seven, and people have seven.

The way that sirtuins were found across species implies they were "saved" with development. Qualities that are "rationed" have all inclusive capacities in numerous or all species. What was at this point to be known, however, was the means by which significant sirtuins would end up being.

In 1991, Elysium fellow benefactor and MIT scholar Leonard Guarente, nearby alumni understudies Nick Austriaco and Brian Kennedy, led trials to all the more likely see how yeast matured. By some coincidence, Austriaco attempted to develop societies of different yeast strains from tests he had put away in his ice chest for quite a long time, which made a distressing domain for the strains. Just a portion of these strains could develop from here, yet Guarente and his group identified an example: The strains of yeast that endure the best in the cooler were likewise the longest lived. This gave direction to Guarente so he could concentrate exclusively on these long-living strains of yeast.

This prompted the identification of SIR2 as a quality that advanced life span in yeast. It's critical to note more research is required on SIR2's belongings in people. The Guarente lab consequently found that expelling SIR2 abbreviated yeast life range significantly, while in particular, expanding the quantity of duplicates of the SIR2 quality from one to two expanded the life length in yeast. In any case, what initiated SIR2 normally presently couldn't seem to be found.

This is the place acetyl bunches become possibly the most important factor. It was at first idea that SIR2 may be a deacetylating protein — which means it expelled those acetyl gatherings — from different atoms, yet nobody knew if this were valid since all endeavors to show this movement in a test tube demonstrated negative. Guarente and his group had the option to find that SIR2 in yeast could just deacetylate different proteins within the sight of the coenzyme NAD+, nicotinamide adenine dinucleotide.

In Guarente's own words: "Without NAD+, SIR2 sits idle. That was the basic finding on the circular segment of sirtuin science."

The Future of Sirtuins

Sirtuins look into has to a great extent been attached to maturing and metabolic movement. "There are possibly 12,000 papers on sirtuins now," Guarente's said. "At the time we found the NAD+ subordinate deacetylase action the quantity of papers was during the 100s."

As the sirtuins field keeps on growing, this leaves space for inconceivable research openings into how enacting sirtuins with NAD+ forerunners can prompt additionally energizing disclosures.

THE RISING INCIDENCE of heftiness related maladies, for example, diabetes, dyslipidemia, and cardiovascular and cerebrovascular infections in industrialized nations has become a general medical issue vital. Numerous helpful and preventive methodologies to forestall or battle stoutness have come around, however few have endure the trial of time. One wonder that got the enthusiasm for this setting is the purported "French mystery." First noted by Irish doctor Samuel Black in 1819, the French Catch 22 makes a mention to the way that the French are seen as having a generally low rate of cardiovascular and metabolic ailment, in spite of the fact that their diet is wealthy in immersed fat. The high utilization of red wine, which is rich in the polyphenol resveratrol, is believed to be one of the essential variables adding to this particular bit of leeway.

In the meantime, since the 1930s, it has been likewise outstanding that caloric limitation (CR) can impede the maturing procedure and postpone the beginning of various maturing related maladies, for example, malignancy, cardiovascular infections, and metabolic illnesses. CR significantly grows lifespan in life forms going from yeast and nematodes to rodents and monkeys (1, 2). Strikingly, the gainful wellbeing results of CR take after those that are incited by resveratrol in various creature models, recommending that the atomic pathways by which resveratrol acts are like those enacted by CR. As of late, it was proposed that the sirtuins could be the normal middle people that clarify both the impacts of resveratrol and CR pathways. In this survey, we will talk about the atomic instrument that underlies the organic action of these sirtuins, their utilitarian jobs in entire body physiology, and their potential relationship to human ailments.

Sirtuins are Nicotinamide Adenine Dinucleotide-Dependent Histone Deacetylases or Adp-Ribosyl Transferases

The establishing individual from the sirtuin protein family was the quiet data controller 2 protein (Sir2p) of Saccharomyces cervisiae, a nicotinamide adenine dinucleotide (NAD+)- subordinate histone deacetylase (HDAC) that directs chromatin hushing (3–7). Yeast strains with unusual degrees of Sir2p show abandons in numerous cell capacities, including transcriptional and recombinational hushing, senescence, and DNA fix. In S. cervisiae, there are four sirtuins (NAD+-subordinate histone deacetylases Hst1–Hst4) notwithstanding Sir2p, while in well evolved creatures seven homologs, for example SIRT1–SIRT7, have been identified (8, 9) (Table 1). The wonderful preservation of individuals from the sirtuin quality family from yeast to people demonstrates that these proteins assume crucial physiological jobs.

Among the huge HDAC protein family, sirtuins were initially sorted as class III HDACs. While classes I and II HDACs use zinc as a cofactor and are repressed by trichostatin A (10), sirtuins are not restrained by trichostatin An and convert acetylated protein substrates in a response that utilizations NAD+ into a deacetylated protein, nicotinamide, and the acetyl ester metabolites 2'-O-and 3'-O-acetyl-ADP ribose (AADPR), which are shaped by the exchange of the acetyl gathering to the ADP-ribose segment of NAD+ (6, 7, 11–14) (Fig. 1). The deacetylase action of the sirtuins is constrained by the cell [NAD+]/[NADH] proportion, for example NAD+ works as an activator, while nicotinamide and diminished nicotinamide adenine dinucleotide (NADH) restrain their action.

Since sirtuins are class III HDACs, it was sensible that their capacity at first became related with transcriptional constraint. Acetylated histones H1, H3, and H4 are known to be physiological substrates for the sirtuins, and lysine 16 in histone H4 has all the earmarks of being the most basic buildup for sirtuin-interceded transcriptional quieting (20, 21). A short time later, it has been perceived that a developing number of nonhistone proteins are additionally deacetylated by the sirtuins, to a great extent extending their organic jobs. These nonhistone sirtuin substrates incorporate a few transcriptional controllers, for example, the atomic factor-κB (NFκB), forkhead box type O translation factors (FOXO), and the peroxisome proliferator-initiated receptor γ (PPARγ) coactivator 1α (PGC-1α), yet in addition chemicals, for example, acetyl coenzyme A (CoA) synthetase 2 (AceCS2), and basic proteins, for example, α-tubulin.

Curiously, AADPR, an item created in the deacetylation response catalyzed by the sirtuins, additionally has a job as a second delivery person since it is engaged with building up a transcriptionally quiet and practically heterochromatic state (20, 22). AADPR accomplishes this impact by two free instruments that include from one viewpoint a conformational change in SIRT1, which in a feedforward circle potentiates the quality quieting impacts of the Sir complex (20), and then again, by official to the histone variation full scale H2A1.1, which is available in idle heterochromatic locales (22). Since cell [NAD+]/[NADH] proportion, nicotinamide, and AADPR levels are administered by cell energetics, SIRT1 might be an amazingly flexible vitality sensor that empowers translation to detect the metabolic condition of the cell.

Two sirtuins, SIRT4 and SIRT6, are missing significant deacetylase movement however rather have a strong NAD+-subordinate ADP-ribosyl transferase action (Fig. 1). The ADP-ribosyl transferase exercises of these two SIRTs are not a total shock in perspective on the underlying report on the enzymatic movement of yeast Sir2p, which depicted a mono-ADP-ribosyl transferase action (23). Posttranslational modification of protein substrates by mono-ADP-ribosylation includes the making of a N-or S-glycosidic linkage between a specific amino corrosive, (for example, arginine or cysteine) on the acceptor protein and the ADP-ribose buildup of NAD+.

33

The seven mammalian sirtuins show significant arrangement homology and contain preserved synergist and NAD+ restricting spaces (Fig. 2 and Table 1). Albeit dependent on succession likenesses, eukaryotic sirtuins have been isolated into four wide phylogenetic gatherings, with SIRT1, SIRT2, and SIRT3 creating class I, SIRT4 establishing class II, SIRT5 shaping class III, and SIRT6 and SIRT7 framing class IV (9), there is no undeniable relationship between's this classification and the specific natural elements of the sirtuins. Another progressively applicable approach to practically classify the sirtuins depends on their intracellular restrictions (24) (Table 1). Four sirtuins, SIRT1, SIRT3, SIRT6, and SIRT7, are atomic proteins, yet their subnuclear limitations are unmistakable. SIRT1 is distinguished in the cores however is avoided from the nucleoli, while SIRT6 and SIRT7, are related with heterochromatic locales and nucleoli, individually (24, 25). SIRT2 is commonly limited in the cytoplasm, yet, during the G2/M stage, it ties chromatin in the core (26). SIRT3, SIRT4, and SIRT5 are available in the mitochondria. Albeit at first portrayed as a mitochondrial protein, ongoing investigations recommend that SIRT3 can likewise be an atomic protein that moves to the mitochondria during cell stress (119). The specific restriction of the SIRT3–SIRT5 in the mitochondria has, in any case, not yet been characterized tentatively.

Each of the seven sirtuins are pervasively communicated in human tissues, albeit more significant levels of mRNA articulation are distinguished in the cerebrum and testis for most sirtuins (8, 24). With the exception of SIRT2 and SIRT5, the articulation for the sirtuins is higher in fetal comparative with grown-up mind, which may demonstrate the likelihood that they assume significant jobs in the improvement of the neuronal framework.

Sirtuins and the Control of Cell Proliferation, Stress Resistance, and Cancer

Numerous components that control cell proliferation and apoptosis are identified as sirtuin substrates, for example, p53 (27–29). SIRT1 is accounted for to be related with the tumor silencer protein p53. p53 has a few acetylation locales, and its hyperacetylation balances out and actuates it to trigger apoptosis and cell-cycle capture (30–32). On the other hand, the deacetylation of p53 by SIRT1 is anticipated to instigate its pulverization by the MDM2 (mouse twofold moment 2)-subordinate ubiquitin-intervened pathway. Truth be told, overexpression of SIRT1 represses p53 transcriptional movement and p53-subordinate apoptosis in light of DNA harm and oxidative pressure, though overexpression of predominant negative SIRT1 protein can potentiate these cell stress reactions (28, 29). In thymocytes from SIRT1-inadequate mice, the degrees of p53 acetylation were significantly up-controlled after presentation to ionizing radiation (33), showing that SIRT1 has a job in expanding the pressure opposition of cells. Expanded p53 acetylation has likewise been related with senescence (34). Strikingly, SIRT1 was indicated as of late to advance replicative senescence, through a procedure that ensnares p19ARF, which emphatically directs p53 through restraining

MDM2 (35). This impact is in stamped differentiation to Sir2p work in yeast, which broadens replicative lifespan.

Sirtuins likewise influence the movement of the FOXO group of translation factors (38, 39). Hereditary epistasis in Caenorhabditis elegans and metabolic investigations in mice demonstrate that FOXO qualities direct cell differentiation, change, and digestion (40). In C. elegans, change of the FOXO ortholog Daf16 (anomalous dauer arrangement) protects the dauer state, brought about by transformations of the insulin/IGF receptor ortholog Daf2 (41–43). In mammalian cells, development factor-prompted initiation of phosphatidylinositol 3-kinase prompts an expansion in the movement of the serine/threonine kinase AKT/protein kinase B (44, 45), which thusly prompts phosphorylation and inactivation of the FOXO proteins by their maintenance in the cytoplasm (46–49). The translocation of FOXO3a from the cytoplasm to the core is instigated by its deacetylation by SIRT1 because of oxidative pressure (50).

SIRT1 is also reported to play an important role during myocyte differentiation. The levels of SIRT1 and the [NAD+]/[NADH] ratio decrease during muscle differentiation. Overexpression of SIRT1 retards muscle differentiation via formation of a complex with the acetyltransferase PCAF (p300/CBP-associated factor) and MyoD, whereas in cells with reduced SIRT1 expression, muscle gene expression and differentiation are enhanced (52). In addition, the muscle cell transcription factor, myocyte enhancer factor MEF2 is inactivated through deacetylation by SIRT1 (53). SIRT1 also was reported to bind and deacetylate the androgen receptor (AR) at a conserved lysine motif, thereby repressing the ligand-induced AR transcriptional activity by the inhibition of coactivator-induced interactions between the AR amino and carboxyl termini.

Hst2, the yeast ortholog of SIRT2 can induce Sir2p-independent lifespan extension and rDNA silencing in yeast, highlighting the redundancies of the SIRTs in the control of lifespan in yeast. As to the mammalian SIRT2, it deacetylates a number of substrates, including α-tubulin and histone H4K16Ac. In mammalian cell culture systems, SIRT2 was shown to play an important role in the control of the cell cycle. The global levels of H4K16 acetylation peak at the S and G2 phase, dropping before cells enter mitosis, coinciding with the increased expression of SIRT2, its nuclear translocation, and association with chromatin). In SIRT2-deficient mouse embryonic fibroblasts (MEFs), H4K16 acetylation remains high during mitosis, delaying S-phase entry. This suggests that the SIRT2-mediated conversion of H4K16Ac to its deacetylated form may be pivotal to the formation of condensed chromatin. SIRT2 has also been suggested to act as a tumor suppressor gene in human gliomas (58). Down-regulation of SIRT2 gene expression and/or deletion of the chromosomal region harboring the SIRT2 gene is frequently observed in gliomas. SIRT2 expression might hence serve as a potential diagnostic molecular marker for gliomas, and modulation of its activity might be of interest for the management of gliomas.

The nuclear protein SIRT6 is a weak deacetylase but is endowed with a robust ADP-ribosyltransferase activity. SIRT6−/− MEFs have an increased frequency of various chromosomal aberrations, which indicates that SIRT6 is involved in maintaining genome integrity. SIRT6 deficiency also impairs the proliferation of these MEFs and enhances their sensitivity to DNA-damaging agents. This regulation of genomic stability by SIRT6 is related to its function in base excision repair (BER) of single-stranded DNA breaks. Interestingly, overexpression of the DNA polymerase involved in BER, Polβ, rescues these defects. SIRT6−/− mice die prematurely subsequent to several rather acute degenerative processes, including loss of sc fat, reduction of bone mineral density, colitis, and lymphopenia associated with increased lymphocyte apoptosis (25). SIRT6 may also control metabolism, because SIRT6−/− mice exhibits low levels of serum IGF-I and a gradual decrease of serum glucose. It remains, however, unclear how SIRT6 influences BER and whether the altered serum IGF and insulin levels of SIRT6−/− mice directly contribute to aging-like phenotypes or, alternatively, reflect compensatory changes.

SIRT7 is a nucleolar protein that is associated with active rRNA genes in which it interacts with RNA polymerase I (61). SIRT7 overexpression increases rRNA transcription, whereas its down-regulation decreases rRNA transcription. Interestingly, SIRT7 expression is enriched in tissues with a high proliferation potential, such as liver, spleen, and testis. This is in contrast to tissues with a low cellular turnover rate, such as skeletal and heart muscle and brain that express low levels of SIRT7. SIRT7 seems hence to drive ribosome biogenesis in dividing cells, and it has been associated with thyroid and breast cancer (62, 63). SIRT7 gene expression is up-regulated in these cancers, and, moreover, its levels are closely related to tumor development and disease progression of breast cancer. Additional study will, however, be required to identify the mechanism underlying enhanced SIRT7 gene expression in these cancers.

All of these studies combined suggest important roles of the sirtuins in the control of cell proliferation: SIRT1 inhibits p53 and modulates FOXO activity, SIRT2 controls chromosome condensation during the cell cycle, SIRT6 acts in BER, whereas SIRT7 activates rRNA transcription.

Sirtuins Control Metabolic Activity

The fact that several of the protein substrates, such as AceCS2 and PGC-1α, which are deacetylated by the sirtuins, are involved in metabolism indicated a metabolic role for this protein family (64–67). This hypothesis was substantiated through studies that used both cell-based approaches as well as a combination of whole animal genetic and pharmacological approaches.

Two groups reported the phenotypes of germ-line SIRT1−/− mice, which showed some similarities but also revealed differences, potentially the result from the methods used to generate the mice (33, 68). In general, SIRT1−/− mice were smaller at birth and showed an elevated postnatal lethality attributable to developmental problems that are not observed in yeast, C. elegans, or Drosophila. In an outbred background, some of the SIRT1−/− mice survived to adulthood, but they have fertility problems and display a variety of other problems, including skeletal, eye, and cardiac defects. The study of some of these genetically engineered SIRT1 mouse models revealed a role of SIRT1 in pancreatic homeostasis. In the pancreas, SIRT1 was preferentially localized in the islets of Langerhans. In the SIRT1−/− mice, insulin secretion in response to glucose was lower compared with wild-type littermates, indicating that SIRT1 positively regulates insulin secretion in pancreatic β-cells (69). Conversely, β-cell-specific SIRT1-overexpressing transgenic mice exhibit an improved glucose tolerance and an enhanced glucose-stimulated insulin secretion (70). From the microarray analysis comparing gene expression patterns in SIRT1-overexpressing- and knockdown pancreatic β-cell lines, uncoupling protein 2 (UCP2), a protein that negatively regulates insulin secretion in pancreatic β-cells, was identified as a target that was repressed by SIRT1. SIRT1 decreases UCP2 gene expression by directly binding to the UCP2 promoter, leading to a better coupling of mitochondrial respiration and ATP synthesis, which will induce insulin secretion.

PPARγ is a key controller in adipogenesis and fat stockpiling through the control of the outflow of numerous adipocyte-specific qualities (71). SIRT1 quells PPARγ effectively by means of docking with two of its corepressors, NcoR (atomic receptor corepressor) and SMRT (quieting go between of retinoid and thyroid hormone receptor). Consequently, SIRT1 was recommended to go about as a corepressor

40

of PPARγ-interceded translation. From a practical perspective, the constraint of PPARγ by SIRT1 weakens adipogenesis, and up-guideline of SIRT1 triggers lipolysis and loss of fat in differentiated fat cells (72). On the other hand, the decrease in SIRT1 articulation in SIRT1+/− mice thus bargains the assembly of unsaturated fats from fat tissue during fasting.

Maybe the most important objective of SIRT1 in the metabolic field is the cofactor PGC-1α, the ace controller of mitochondrial biogenesis. PGC-1α is initiated by SIRT1-intervened deacetylation (65, 66). In the liver, the initiation of PGC-1α will encourage the gluconeogenic movement of hepatocyte atomic factor 4α and invigorate hepatic glucose yield (66). In the muscle and darker fat tissue (BAT), the SIRT1-intervened deacetylation of PGC-1α is converted into improved mitochondrial action, which interpreted in expanded exercise resistance and thermogenesis, prompting security against the beginning of weight and related metabolic brokenness (73). For its deacetylase action, SIRT1 is carefully reliant on cell NAD+ levels, which reflect cell vitality status. The progressions in cell NAD+ levels that influence SIRT1 deacetylase action subsequently appear to advise PGC-1α about the cell vitality status. PGC-1α would then be able to adjust cell vitality creation through its instructing job on mitochondrial biogenesis and capacity. These examinations place SIRT1, which goes about as cell vitality sensor, upstream of PGC-1α as a significant controller of mitochondrial movement.

Obviously a significant number of these examinations, which concentrated on a given tissue type, showed potential connections between metabolic homeostasis and SIRT1 activity. As talked about, SIRT1 improves insulin discharge because of glucose in the pancreas through the constraint of UCP2 (69, 70); in the liver, SIRT1 incites gluconeogenesis and stifles glycolysis (66); in fat tissue, SIRT1 restrains fat stockpiling and increments lipolysis by means of restraint of PPARγ (72). These pleiotropic, often contradicting, metabolic impacts of SIRT1 in different tissues convoluted the explanation of the effect of SIRT1 on entire body metabolic homeostasis. Two late examinations utilizing the SIRT1 activator resveratrol shed all the more light on this mind boggling job of SIRT1 in digestion (73, 74). In one examination, it was demonstrated that resveratrol emulates a few parts of CR in mice on a fatty diet, by dragging out lifespan, improving insulin affectability, and upgrading engine work (74). This examination thus broadens past work that SIRT1 initiation by resveratrol imitates CR and postpones maturing in a wide scope of living beings going from S. cerevisiae (75) over C. elegans to Drosophila (76). In a subsequent autonomous investigation, treatment of mice with a higher portion of resveratrol was likewise appeared to secure them against diet-instigated heftiness and the related insulin opposition (73). This investigation showed that the improvement of insulin affectability was connected to an upgraded mitochondrial work ensuing to actuation of PGC-1α by SIRT1-intervened PGC-1α deacetylation (73). The improved mitochondrial movement moreover prompted an expansion in oxidative sort muscle filaments and

42

upgraded protection from muscle weariness. In addition, a significant relationship between three single-nucleotide polymorphisms in the SIRT1 quality and vitality homeostasis in people demonstrated that SIRT1 establishes an alluring and approved objective to manage vitality and metabolic homeostasis in man (73).

SIRT3 was initially thought to be a mitochondrial protein, however as of late it was shown that mitochondrial move from its typical atomic area was initiated during cell stress (77, 78, 119). The statement of SIRT3 is finely controlled. In mice, caloric limitation (CR) up-controls SIRT3 articulation levels in white fat tissue and BAT. Moreover, chilly presentation additionally actuates SIRT3 in BAT (79). Strikingly, the constitutive articulation of SIRT3 advances the statement of PGC-1α, UCP1, and different qualities associated with mitochondrial capacities, demonstrating that SIRT3 balances versatile thermogenesis in BAT, a procedure that probably includes both atomic and mitochondrial exercises. One mitochondrial movement of SIRT3 is the deacetylation and actuation of the mitochondrial type of AceCS2, a catalyst that catalyzes the development of acetyl CoA from acetic acid derivation (64, 67). Deacetylation of AceCS2 consequently expands the transformation of acetic acid derivation into acetyl CoA, a halfway of the tricarboxylic corrosive cycle. AceCS2 is copiously communicated in heart and skeletal muscle yet missing from liver, and its demeanor is actuated when vitality gets constraining, as during CR and ketogenesis (80). Since SIRT3 encourages the metabolic utilization of acetic acid derivation, it might thus be particularly essential to guarantee vitality generation under conditions when ATP is rare (64, 67, 80). In similarity to this capacity of SIRT3, SIRT1 deacetylates and enacts the cytoplasmic AceCS1 to give acetyl CoA, which goes about as a structure hinder for unsaturated fat and cholesterol blend (64). For just one of the human sirtuins, for example SIRT3, a direct hereditary connection with life span has been built up. Truth be told, changes in the SIRT3 quality enhancer, which up-control its appearance, were improved in extensive people (81).

Another mitochondrial SIRT protein, SIRT4, was indicated as of late to collaborate with glutamate dehydrogenase (GDH) (82). Glutamate shaped from glutamine is changed over to the tricarboxylic corrosive cycle moderate α-ketoglutarate by GDH in the mitochondria (82, 83). This advances mitochondrial enactment and expands the ATP/ADP proportion, which consequently initiates insulin discharge in pancreatic β-cells. SIRT4 utilizes NAD+ to ADP-ribosylate and decline the action of GDH, therefore decreasing the creation of α-ketoglutarate and the age of ATP (82). In SIRT4-inadequate pancreatic β-cells, GDH movement expands, prompting an incitement of insulin emission in light of glutamine. SIRT4 therefore inhibitorily affects amino corrosive invigorated insulin emission (AASIS). It appears to be sensible to conjecture that AASIS is initiated during ceaseless CR, since protein turnover is expanded and amino acids are utilized as carbon and vitality sources to drive gluconeogenesis in this condition. Steady with this, SIRT4 suppression of GDH is eased during long haul

CR, bringing about enactment of AASIS in β-cells and conceivably gluconeogenesis in liver. CR consequently diminishes SIRT4 movement, which is against the acceptance of SIRT1 action during CR. Besides, SIRT4 and SIRT1 apply, individually, a negative and positive control on insulin emission, which is striking given that their exercises are both constrained by a solitary metabolite, for example NAD+.

Sirtuins in Neural Protection and Neurodegenerative Diseases

Axonal degeneration is a significant morphological trademark seen in both fringe neuropathies and neurodegenerative infections, for example, Alzheimer's illness (AD) and amyotrophic parallel sclerosis (84, 85). Axonal degeneration as a rule happens in the beginning period in degenerative procedures and often goes before or connects intimately with clinical side effects, for example, subjective decrease. There are a few reports that help an axonal defensive job for SIRT1 in the neuronal framework. A pointless degeneration process is seen at the distal segment of a transected axon, which is called Wallerian degeneration (86). Wallerian degeneration moderate (wlds) is a mouse line with postponed axonal degeneration because of axonal damage (87–89). This wonder is believed to be gotten from overexpression of an illusory atomic particle (Wlds protein) that relates to the full-length nicotinamide mononucleotide adenyltransferase 1 (Nmnat 1), a chemical required for both the anew and rescue pathways of NAD+ biosynthesis (90–92) (Fig. 3), and a short area of a ubiquitin combination corruption protein 2a. In an ongoing report,

45

overexpression of Nmnat 1 alone could forestall axonal degeneration, demonstrating that the defensive impact of Nmnat 1 could be interceded by an expansion of neuronal NAD+ save as well as SIRT1 movement.

Superpathway of NAD+ Biosynthesis in Mammals NAD+ is combined through two significant pathways, the again and rescue pathways, and these two pathways merge at nicotinic corrosive mononucleotide. In the again pathway, the nicotinic corrosive moiety of NAD+ is blended from tryptophan by means of the kynurenine pathway. In the NAD+ rescue pathway, NAD+ is created through the reusing of its debasement item, for example, nicotinamide. Craftsmanship, ADP-ribosyl transferase; NA, nicotinic corrosive; NAAD, nicotinic corrosive adenine dinucleotide; NAM, nicotinamide; NaMN, nicotinic corrosive mononucleotide; Nampt, nicotinamide phosphoribosyltransferase; NMN, nicotinamide mononucleotide; NPT, nicotinic corrosive phosphoribosyltransferase; NR, nicotinamide riboside; Nrk, nicotinamide riboside kinase; PARP, poly-ADP-polymerases; PBEF, pre-B cell settlement upgrading factor.

It is outstanding that CR shields neurons from degeneration in mouse models of AD and Parkinson's malady, and SIRT1 may encourage neuronal endurance (94–97). In spite of the fact that it is accounted for that caloric admission and insulin affectability are connected to AD, the system hidden these associations are not completely clarified starting at yet (98, 99). The pathology of AD is described by the nearness of amyloid plaques, intracellular neurofibrillary tangles, and articulated cell passing (100). The amyloid plaque is made out of amyloid-β (Aβ) peptide, which is divided from the amyloid forerunner protein consecutively by β-secretase and γ-secretase (101–103). This irregular Aβ peptide testimony inside the mind is the sign of AD neuropathology, and amassing of collected Aβ is conjectured to start an obsessive course bringing about the beginning and movement of AD (104). Aβ peptides can initiate NFκB movement in microglia by means of TNF-receptor type 1 or receptor of cutting edge glycation finished result (105, 106). SIRT1 enactment or the organization of the SIRT1 activator resveratrol extraordinarily lessens this NFκB flagging (107). This emphatically proposes SIRT1 can lessen Aβ-invigorated neurotoxicity and AD-related fiery reactions by means of hindrance of microglial NFκB flagging. SIRT1 is moreover expected to forestall Aβ peptide age through advancement of the nonamyloidogenic preparing of amyloid antecedent protein by the restraint of Rho kinase 1 articulation.

Notwithstanding this incendiary course prompting neuronal cell demise, another natural cell passing pathway, for example mitochondria-based cell demise pathway, is standing out with regards to AD. Truth be told, Aβ peptides, which can legitimately enter the mitochondrial internal film, can tie to a mitochondrial-grid protein named Aβ-restricting liquor dehydrogenase and confine to the mitochondria. This decreases ATP creation and builds the age of oxygen radicals, which therefore may incite mitochondria-subordinate cell passing in light of the fact that harmed mitochondria can't keep up

47

the vitality requests of the cells. Predictable with these perceptions, in AD mouse models, a solid relationship among Aβ and the inward mitochondrial layer together with expanded free-radical age and diminished cytochrome c oxidase action has been accounted for (111, 112). SIRT1 could, through its invigorating action on mitochondria (73), add to this procedure in AD.

Additionally in Huntington's illness (HD), another neurodegenerative malady, mitochondrial inadequacy is watched. HD patients are described by stamped decreases in glucose digestion and expanded degrees of lactate in the basal ganglia, by a diminished movement of a few key segments of the oxidative phosphorylation pathways in the mitochondria of the striatal neurons (113) and by articulated morphological variations from the norm, including unhinging of the mitochondrial framework and cristae (114). These mitochondrial dysfunctions should be related with dysregulation of PGC-1α interpretation and additionally movement by the freak huntingtin protein (115–117). Since ongoing reports show that PGC-1α action is managed by SIRT1 (66, 73) and on the grounds that a few parts of mitochondrial digestion are constrained by a portion of the sirtuins, the adjustment of sirtuin movement could be a fascinating methodology for the treatment of these neurodegenerative ailments. Truth be told, the capability of such a technique was approved in nematode HD models and in mouse neuronal cell lines (118). In these models, the extended polyglutamine (PolyQ) track in HD-related protein huntingtin (htt) were appeared to actuate PolyQ-subordinate neuronal brokenness. This variation from the norm brought about by the freak PolyQ could be saved by overexpression of SIRT1 or by resveratrol treatment (118). This good impact was smothered by sirtuin inhibitors, for example, nicotinamide or sirtinol, legitimately demonstrating that SIRT1 initiation could be helpful in HD.

Points of view

The establishing individual from the sirtuin family, Sir2p in yeast or SIRT1 in warm blooded animals, has now been entrenched as a key particle that influences life span inside the setting of CR in a few model life forms running from yeast to mouse, despite the fact that the systems included might be unmistakable in the different species. The imperative job that the sirtuins play in cell metabolic control showed that they could be significant determinants of entire body digestion and secure against numerous interminable maladies related with metabolic brokenness. Moreover, potential uses of the sirtuins in neuronal cell endurance and reaction to stress and cell-cycle control clue to inevitable significance of this quality family in the pathogenesis of neurodegenerative illnesses and malignant growth. Extra understanding into the organic activities of the sirtuins will require the meaning of the specific jobs of every one of the quality relatives in vivo with suitable hereditary, pharmacological, and physiological apparatuses. When this is accomplished, it is normal that a select individual from the sirtuins could become potential intriguing focuses for future treatments against age-related infections.

Cerebrum maturing is described by dynamic loss of neurophysiological capacities that is often joined by age-related neurodegeneration. Calorie limitation has been connected to expansion of lifespan and decrease of the danger of neurodegenerative ailments in trial model frameworks. A few flagging pathways have been shown to underlie the valuable impacts of calorie limitation, among which the sirtuin family has been proposed to assume a focal job. In well evolved creatures, it has been built up that sirtuins manage physiological reactions to digestion and stress, two key factors that influence the way toward maturing. Sirtuins speak to a promising new class of rationed deacetylases that assume a significant job in managing digestion and maturing. This audit centers around current comprehension of the connection between metabolic pathways including sirtuins and the cerebrum maturing process, with center around SIRT1 and SIRT3. Identification of remedial specialists equipped for tweaking the articulation and additionally movement of sirtuins is relied upon to give promising procedures to enhancing neurodegeneration. Future examinations with respect to the purposeful transaction of the different sirtuins will assist us with seeing progressively about the maturing procedure, and possibly lead to the improvement of remedial methodologies for the treatment of age-related neurodegenerative illnesses and advancement of effective maturing.

Presentation

The cerebrum, like different organs, experiences a progressive decrease in vitality digestion during maturing (Drew and

50

Leeuwenburgh, 2004; Navarro and Boveris, 2007; Boveris and Navarro, 2008; Swerdlow, 2011). Since neurons require a lot of vitality for the terminating of activity potential, neurotransmission, and different procedures, the age-related decrease in digestion adds to the intellectual decays related with maturing (Biessels and Kappelle, 2005; Boveris and Navarro, 2008). Maturing is likewise a hazard factor for age-related sicknesses, for example, neurodegenerative issue. These illnesses may happen when neurons neglect to react adaptively to an age-related decrease in basal metabolic rates and in vitality driven undertakings, for example, neuromuscular coordination, subjective execution, and natural mindfulness (Swerdlow, 2007). In the previous decade, the capacity of mammalian sirtuins, developmentally preserved nicotinamide adenine dinucleotide (NAD)- subordinate protein deacetylases/ADP-ribosyltransferases, has been explored in more prominent detail, and we presently have a vastly improved sub-atomic comprehension of the various jobs that this novel group of catalysts plays in maturing and apparently every natural procedure. There is little uncertainty that sirtuins have developed as basic modulators of metabolic versatile reactions, and their exercises have been connected to numerous maladies, from metabolic variations from the norm to neurodegeneration.

Sirtuins were initially identified as one of the qualities that control the mating kinds of growing yeast, Saccharomyces cerevisiae, and named quiet data controller 2 (Sir2) in lower living beings (Klar and Fogel, 1979). Following the main distribution depicting a job for yeast Sir2 in advancing life span (Kaeberlein et al., 1999), numerous examinations concentrated on clarifying whether sirtuins may assume comparable jobs in different life forms. Sirtuins have been appeared to control lifespan in lower living beings, including yeast, nematodes, and natural product flies (Haigis and Guarente, 2006), despite the fact that their job in worm and fly lifespan has as of late been discussed (Burnett et al., 2011; Viswanathan and Guarente, 2011). The majority of these investigations have depicted a key job for SIRT1 in managing the metabolic reaction to calorie limitation (CR; Canto and Auwerx, 2009), a dietary intercession that vigorously broadens life range over various species. In any case, entire body overexpression of SIRT1 in mice doesn't influence life range (Herranz et al., 2010). In any case, SIRT1 appears to advance solid maturing by securing against a few age-related pathologies, for example, encouraging insulin affectability, hoisting glucose generation, diminishing oxidative pressure, potentiating action of mind inferred neurotrophic factor (BDNF) transcriptional factor cAMP reaction component restricting protein (CREB; Guarente and Franklin, 2011).

Well evolved creatures have seven sirtuins (SIRT1–7) which are found in different subcellular areas, including the core (SIRT1, SIRT6, and SIRT7), cytosol (SIRT2), and mitochondria (SIRT3, SIRT4, and SIRT5). A large portion of the examinations have depicted a key job for SIRT1 in controlling the metabolic reaction to CR (Canto and Auwerx, 2009), a dietary routine including decreased 30–40% calorie consumption contrasted with typical calorie admission, that brought about broadened lifespan and diminished improvement of grimness with maturing (Jiang et al., 2000; Masoro, 2000; Sinclair, 2002; Koubova and Guarente, 2003). Calorie limitation is the main intercession that has reliably been appeared to defer the beginning, slow the movement of age-related malady, and broaden lifespan in brief species, just as in extensive non-human primates, recommending that comparative components would be employable in people. Entire body overexpression of Sirt1 in mice doesn't influence lifespan (Herranz et al., 2010). By and by, SIRT1 advances solid maturing by forestalling age-related pathologies (Guarente and Franklin, 2011). Another solid connection between mammalian sirtuins and the counter maturing impacts of CR was given by SIRT3, which intercedes the counteraction of age-related hearing loss (Someya et al., 2010). SIRT3 is required for the CR-intervened decrease of oxidative harm in various tissues through guideline of the glutathione cancer prevention agent framework (Someya et al., 2010).

In this audit, we center around the impacts of SIRT1 and SIRT3 on metabolic guideline and their enemy of maturing movement in cerebrum, and further talk about potential pharmacological ways to deal with cure and forestall age-related neurological issue by focusing on sirtuins.

SIRT1, Metabolism and Brain Aging

Circulation of SIRT1 in the Brain

During mouse embryogenesis, SIRT1 is profoundly communicated in the mind, spinal cord, and dorsal root ganglion, with the pinnacle articulation at E4.5 (Salminen and Kaarniranta, 2012). SIRT1 is likewise communicated in the grown-up cerebrum, with elevated levels in the cortex, hippocampus, cerebellum, and nerve center, and low levels in white issue (Singh, 2004). Among the different cell sorts of mind, SIRT1 is overwhelmingly, if not only, communicated in neurons (Singh, 2004; Adler et al., 2007; Salminen and Kaarniranta, 2012). The main special case is that SIRT1 is found in microglia when co-refined with neurons (Schmitz et al., 2004). At the subcellular level, SIRT1 is seen as an atomic protein (Chen and Greene, 2003). However it is accounted for that SIRT1 has both atomic import and fare arrangements, and that SIRT1 is available in the cytosolic part of mouse cerebrum, in spite of the fact that its cytosolic work is simply starting to be explained (Chen et al., 2005b; Lee et al., 2008; Hardie, 2011).

SIRT1 Mediates Metabolic Benefits Under CR

SIRT1 contains 747 amino acids in people, with an anticipated atomic weight of 81 kDa and a deliberate one of 120 kDa. Notwithstanding histones, SIRT1 likewise deacetylates various non-histone substrates, including p53 (Luo et al., 2001)and peroxisome proliferator-enacted receptor γ (PPARγ) coactivator-1α (PGC-1α; Nemoto et al., 2005), and FOXO (Xiong et al., 2011), atomic factor κ-light-chain-enhancer of initiated B cells (NF-κB; Salminen et al., 2008b). SIRT1 is drawing considerably more consideration since it is viewed as one of the

54

deciding elements in lifespan expansion instigated by CR, a marvel saw in phylogenetically various creatures including yeast, worm, natural product fly, and mouse (Kaeberlein et al., 1999; Tissenbaum and Guarente, 2001; Howitz et al., 2003; Rogina and Helfand, 2004). Its useful jobs are additionally bolstered by the discoveries that putative SIRT1-initiating mixes, for example, resveratrol, likewise advance life span in a few animal varieties, including yeast (Howitz et al., 2003), worm (Wood et al., 2004), and mouse (Baur et al., 2006), making it an enemy of maturing objective.

The impacts of SIRT1 on life span depend on its enzymatic action of deacetylation of histone and non-histone substrates. While the deacetylation of histones prompts their association with DNA and subsequent quality hushing (Braunstein et al., 1993; Sauve et al., 2006; Dali-Youcef et al., 2007), the deacetylation of non-histone proteins has a wide scope of organic impacts, including metabolic change, endurance advancement, and autophagy (Campisi, 2005; Dali-Youcef et al., 2007; Brooks and Gu, 2009; Madeo et al., 2010). For instance, SIRT1 represses p53 (Luo et al., 2001), diminishing its expert apoptotic impact. It likewise restrains NF-κB (Yeung et al., 2004), lessening its genius provocative impacts. Conversely, SIRT1 enacts a transcriptional coactivator, PGC-1α (Nemoto et al., 2005), prompting expanded glucose levels, insulin affectability, and mitochondrial biogenesis. Together, these and different impacts, add to the life span evoked by CR.

These metabolic changes and the cytoprotective association of CR are commonly considered to happen in non-neural organs, for example, the liver, pancreas, muscle, and fat tissues (Brooks and Gu, 2009; Imai and Guarente, 2010). Be that as it may, late examinations recommend that the nerve center may likewise add to the life span impacts of SIRT1 and CR by means of coordination of neurobehavioral and neuroendocrine changes, including internal heat level, craving, and generally physical action (Dietrich et al., 2010; Satoh et al., 2010). SIRT1 is plentifully communicated in a few areas in the nerve center of mice, particularly in the arcuate, paraventricular, ventro-and dorsomedial cores; and CR expands SIRT1 levels in the nerve center, which builds internal heat level, nourishment consumption, and physical movement (Ramadori et al., 2008; Dietrich et al., 2010; Satoh et al., 2010).

It has become progressively obvious that the healthy impacts of the CR, are partially because of the advancement of sirtuins (Wang et al., 2010). The articulation levels of SIRT1 increment upon CR in a few rat and human tissues, including white fat, liver, skeletal muscle, mind, and kidney. Levels of NAD have been appeared to ascend in liver cells under CR-like conditions, which thusly incites articulation of SIRT1 (Rodgers et al., 2005). SIRT1 winds up expending NAD+ because of its deacetylase movement, creating nicotinamide, an inhibitor of its own action. NAD+ is known to ensure neurons (Liu et al., 2009) and in this way by expanding the degrees of NAD+, CR may preserveSIRT1 movement. SIRT1 likewise initiates PGC1α (Rodgers

56

et al., 2005) which results in mitochondrial biogenesis (Liu et al., 2009). A decrease in mitochondrial action is believed to be causative in many age-related sicknesses (Petersen et al., 2003; Singh, 2004). CR summons upgrades in mitochondrial movement like those of SIRT1. Therefore, it is conceivable that little atom modulators of SIRT1 may follow up on indistinguishable pathways from those modified by CR, and in this way can possibly alleviate age-related ailments (Lavu et al., 2008).

SIRT1 communicates with and tweaks other key components engaged with mammalian maturing, for example, NF-κB that controls a second rate fundamental aggravation alongside human maturing process-inflamm-maturing (Salminen et al., 2008a), mammalian objective of rapamycin (mTOR; Finley and Haigis, 2009), AMP-actuated protein kinase (AMPK; Salminen and Kaarniranta, 2012), therefore controls the gin procedure. The maturing procedure includes changes in insusceptible guideline; NF-κB flagging is the ace controller of the safe framework. Restraint of NF-κB motioning in matured mice returned the tissue attributes and worldwide quality articulation to those of youthful mice (Adler et al., 2007). The capacity of the NFκB complex can be controlled by the acetylation of the p65 part (Schmitz et al., 2004). SIRT1 can associate with RelA/p65 protein in the NF-κB complex and specifically deacetylates lysine 310, which has been exhibited to potentiate the transactivation limit of the NFκB complex (Chen and Greene, 2003). A few examinations have shown that SIRT1 is a powerful inhibitor of NF-κB interpretation (Yeung et al., 2004;

Chen et al., 2005b). The flagging connection among SIRT1 and NF-κB is particularly intriguing as for maturing, as an outcome of the arrival of the SIRT1 brake, the transactivation effectiveness of NF-κB factor is potentiated, which brings out insusceptible actuation and inflamm-maturing.

Maturing process is additionally controlled via autophagy. It has been identified the flagging pathways that direct autophagic corruption and SIRT1 is an intense controller of autophagic debasement (Lee et al., 2008), SIRT1 can associate with and deacetylates a few parts in the buildings of framing autophagosomes, for example, Atg5, Atg7, and Atg8 proteins (Lee et al., 2008). There is an unmistakable cover between the flagging networks managing both maturing and autophagocytosis, which accentuates the significant job of autophagy in the directing of maturing and age-related degenerative infections. It is apparent that expansion in autophagy can expand lifespan. mTOR action is stifled by CR, decrease in mTOR flagging is a rationale applicant system for the counter maturing advantages of CR. Through deacetylation of an assortment of proteins associated with autophagy process, SIRT1 can manage physiological procedure during maturing and directed by CR (Haigis and Guarente, 2006).

Productive control of vitality metabolic homeostasis is a sign of improved healthspan and broadened lifespan. The AMPK and SIRT1 flagging pathways are exceptionally monitored vitality sensor of expanded degrees of AMP and NAD+, separately, AMPK flagging is engaged with the guideline of vitality metabolic homeostasis (Hardie,

2011). Canto and Auwerx (2009) exhibited that the initiation of AMPK invigorated the utilitarian movement of SIRT1 by expanding the intracellular grouping of NAD+. Curiously, SIRT1 had the option to deacetylate LKB1 kinase which consequently expanded its movement (Lan et al., 2008). Since LKB1 is an upstream activator of AMPK, this flagging pathway animates the enactment of AMPK. This positive criticism circle among SIRT1 and AMPK can likewise potentiate the capacity of the other AMPK-initiated flagging pathways. The cozy connection among AMPK and SIRT1 is proof that vitality balance successfully controls cell reactions by means of a coordinated flagging network. AMPK can repress the movement of mTOR complex by means of two different instruments, either by legitimately phosphorylating the Raptor, an administrative segment of mTORC1, or by the phosphorylation of tuberous sclerosis protein 2 (TSC2), which in this manner smothers the action of mTOR (Jung et al., 2010; Mihaylova and Shaw, 2011). Taken together, SIRT1 connects with other key enemy of maturing flagging pathways consequently adding to life span control.

It has been set up that maturing is a realized hazard factor for some, neurodegenerative sicknesses including Alzheimer's malady (AD), Parkinson's ailment (PD), Wallerian neurodegeneration, Huntington's illness (HD), and amyotrophic sidelong sclerosis (ALS). The pathomechanisms associated with these disarranges include regular biochemical pathways and procedures, including protein misfolding, oligomerization, and collection, proteolysis, post-translational modifications, mitochondrial brokenness, anomalous metabolic procedures, and proinflammatory and proapoptotic reactions that we examine in the following area.

SIRT1 and Age-Associated Neurological Diseases

Wallerian degeneration

Wallerian degeneration alludes to axonal passing and debasement after central damage, trailed by breakdown of myelin sheath. The neuroprotective impact of SIRT1 against Wallerian degeneration was first found in wlds transgenic mice (Perry et al., 1990). These mice showed a significant deferral in axonal degeneration after physical or substance damage. The unthinking reason for the postponed axonal harm was evidently connected with the freak wlds fanciful protein. It has been indicated that Nicotinamide mononucleotide adenylyltransferase 1 (NMNAT-1) movement assumes a significant job in the counteraction of axonal harm, applying its defensive impacts through SIRT1 actuation, as the neuroprotection is hindered by the SIRT1 inhibitor sirtinol or siRNA-interceded SIRT1 hushing (Araki et al., 2004; Sasaki et al., 2009; Babetto et al., 2010). The job of SIRT1 stays questionable, be that as it may, as both SIRT1-subordinate (Araki et al., 2004) and - free instruments are accounted for (Wang et al., 2005b).

Alzheimer's malady

Alzheimer's malady is a terminal neurodegenerative ailment, causing neuronal demise and mind decay. The obsessive signs of AD are the

60

intracellular tangles and extracellular plaques in mind. The tangles, otherwise called neurofibrillary tangles, are framed by collection of insoluble tau proteins, and the plaques are stores of β-amyloid (Aβ) peptides, ordinarily comprising of 40–42 amino corrosive buildups.

The defensive impact of SIRT1 against AD was at first seen in CR examines, where CR decreased Aβ and plaque age in the cerebrums of transgenic AD mice (Patel et al., 2005; Wang et al., 2005a). Additionally, the decrease of Aβ was likewise seen in the cortex of fasted squirrel monkeys and is conversely corresponded with SIRT1 levels (Qin et al., 2006a). These examinations infer that SIRT1 is engaged with neuroprotection against AD. Without a doubt, late investigations exhibit that SIRT1 initiation diminishes the neuronal passing and cerebrum decay that are normal for AD (Chen et al., 2005b; Qin et al., 2006b; Kim et al., 2007; Donmez et al., 2010; Min et al., 2010). SIRT1 inadequacy is related with expanded degrees of phosphorylated-tau in neurons (Min et al., 2010) and the measure of neurofibrillary tangles in AD cerebrums (Julien et al., 2009).

Additionally, ongoing investigations show that either organization of resveratrol or overexpression of SIRT1 diminishes Aβ levels both in vitro and in vivo (Chen et al., 2005b; Qin et al., 2006b; Donmez et al., 2010). SIRT1 overexpression animates the creation of α-secretase in neurons and mice by two pathways: enacting the retinoic corrosive receptor (RAR; Donmez et al., 2010) and hindering the rho-related, looped curl containing protein kinase 1 (ROCK1; Qin et al., 2006b). Expanded degrees of α-secretase improve typical procedure of

Amyloid antecedent protein (APP), prompting diminished age of harmful Aβ. Likewise, SIRT1 additionally lessens the NF-kappaB pathway in microglia and diminishes Aβ level (Chen et al., 2005b). Taken together, these outcomes set up that SIRT1 ensures against AD by various systems, including debasement of tau and diminishing degrees of Aβ.

Parkinson's malady

Parkinson's malady is a typical neurodegenerative illness brought about by the passing of dopaminergic neurons of the substantia nigra in the midbrain. The significant indications of PD are unbending nature, tremor, and bradykinesia. Our initial examination found that CR or utilization of 2-deoxy-D-glucose, a glucose simple, diminishes the loss of dopaminergic neurons in mice and improves engine work, suggesting that SIRT1 might be engaged with the security (Duan and Mattson, 1999). The degrees of SIRT1 in dopaminergic neurons are pointedly diminished by treatment with neurotoxins, for example, rotenone, 6-hydroxydopamine, α-synuclein, or 1-methyl-4-phenyl-1,2,3,6-tetrahydropyridine (MPTP; Alvira et al., 2007; Pallas et al., 2008; Albani et al., 2009), which are specialists generally used to demonstrate PD. Furthermore, SIRT1 overexpression (Wareski et al., 2009) or enactment by resveratrol (Okawara et al., 2007; Chao et al., 2008; Albani et al., 2009) eases back neuronal passing just as neurodegeneration in PD models both in vivo and in vitro (Donmez et al., 2012), showing a neuroprotective job of SIRT1 against PD. Not all examinations indicated a defensive job of SIRT1, nonetheless. For instance, no security was seen in a MPTP-actuated PD model in SIRT1 transgenic mice (Kakefuda et al., 2009). In any case, in spite of the debate, most research exhibits a defensive job of SIRT1 against PD, despite the fact that the instruments are hazy.

Huntington's malady

Huntington's malady is an autosomal prevailing inherited ailment with beginning in middle-age. It is brought about by a trinucleotide rehash transformation in the huntingtin quality that outcomes in an expanded number of glutamine deposits in the N-end of the huntingtin protein which causes anomalous protein conglomeration and at last neuronal demise. Our past examination demonstrated that CR could enhance the engine phenotype and broaden endurance of HD mice (Duan et al., 2003), showing that pathways identified with vitality digestion can modify ailment movement in the infection. CR increments mitochondrial biogenesis by actuating endothelial nitric oxide synthase (eNOS), and NO can initiate the SIRT1 quality (Nisoli et al., 2005; Haigis and Guarente, 2006), which is the mammalian ortholog of yeast Sir2, and a profoundly moderated NAD+-subordinate protein deacetylase. Besides, SIRT1 has been recommended to intercede some valuable impacts of CR (Canto and Auwerx, 2009; Wakeling et al., 2009; Shimokawa and Trindade, 2010; Chalkiadaki and Guarente, 2012).

The primary report showing the association among SIRT1 and HD originated from contemplates by Parker et al. (2005), who found that overexpression of Sir2.1 or treatment with resveratrol protected neuronal brokenness phenotypes actuated by freak polyglutamine in Caenorhabditis elegans. As opposed to the neuroprotective impact of Sir2.1 in C. elegans, Pallos et al. (2008) revealed that half decrease of Sir2 broadened endurance and protected neurons containing photoreceptor in flies communicating freak Htt. Strikingly, in the fly model framework, overexpression of Sir2 doesn't diminish the lethality or the degree of neuronal degeneration brought about by freak Htt. Concentrates in both C. elegans and Drosophila recommend that total loss of Sir2 is injurious in the worm (Parker et al., 2005) and is malicious contrasted and heterozygous loss in freak Htt-tested flies (Pallos et al., 2008). Albeit heterozygous loss of Sir2 is defensive in flies, heterozygous loss of Sir2 in worms was not analyzed. All things considered, decrease of Sir2 neither modifies the life-range of flies not communicating Htt nor kin communicating Htt. A few parts of the job of sirtuins in lifespan in C. elegans and Drosophila are dubious, and examines have shown that Sir2 overexpression didn't expand lifespan and that dietary limitation expanded lifespan in flies autonomously of dSir2 (Burnett et al., 2011). In any case, overexpression of Sir2 builds the life span of typical flies and the life span of unhealthy flies is somewhat expanded by raised Sir2 (Pallos et al., 2008). The different outcomes may be because of the measure of Sir2, its initiation status, and different downstream targets included. These questionable outcomes warrant further examination of the job of SIRT1 in mammalian frameworks.

Without a doubt, two autonomous investigations by our gathering (Jiang et al., 2011) and Krainc's gathering (Jeong et al., 2011) showed that balancing the degrees of SIRT1 has helpful advantage in three different HD mouse models, and putative downstream focuses of SIRT1 associated with improved illness results are likewise identified. These two investigations give convincing help to the view that SIRT1 gives advantageous impacts in HD mouse models, yet in addition bring up significant issues. It is conceivable that the conflicting outcomes on the impacts of SIRT1 in models of HD may be clarified by different effector pathways or systems and by setting subordinate impacts or different degrees of SIRT1 actuation. SIRT1 has various targets, and different models of HD show different phenotypes by initiating different targets and systems. Therefore, it isn't amazing to watch conflicting information, particularly in different species and different models.

Amyotrophic Lateral Sclerosis

Amyotrophic horizontal sclerosis is an incessant, lethal neurodegenerative malady, described pathologically by the demise of engine neurons in the spinal cord and cortex, perhaps incited by a lack in the compound superoxide dismutase 1 (SOD1; Rosen, 1993). In the creature model of ALS where a freak type of SOD1 is communicated, SIRT1 levels are upregulated in engine neurons (Kim et al., 2007). SIRT1 overexpression secures neurons against poisonous quality prompted by the freak SOD1 in both refined neurons and mouse mind (Kim et al., 2007). This assurance compares to the expanded deacetylation of p53. Resveratrol additionally upgrades the defensive impact of SIRT1 in a mouse model of ALS (Kim et al., 2007; Markert et al., 2010), however various dosages are give off an impression of being important to improve neurological capacity and increment the life span of mice (Markert et al., 2010).

Various sclerosis

Various sclerosis is a myelin sheath infection with sores normally situated in the mind, spinal cord or cranial nerves, and, most generally, in the optic nerve. The reasons for various sclerosis are not completely identified yet likely emerge from an immune system etiology; therefore, it is generally treated as a fiery sickness. As of late, notwithstanding, numerous sclerosis has likewise been viewed as a neurodegenerative infection in light of the concurrence of lasting axonal harm, neuronal loss, and neurological inability in patients with the sickness (Lassmann, 2010; Shindler et al., 2010). In a mouse model of different sclerosis, test immune system encephalomyelitis (EAE), SIRT1 initiation by SRT501 or SRT1720 keeps up axonal thickness, forestalls neuronal loss, and improves neuronal brokenness (Shindler et al., 2007, 2010). SIRT1 hindrance with Sirtinol constricts the neuroprotective impacts of SRT501 (Shindler et al., 2010), proposing a defensive job of SIRT1 in numerous sclerosis. In any case, further examinations are important to completely portray the job of SIRT1 in various sclerosis.

Cerebral ischemia

Ischemic stroke is a typical neurological illness brought about by the abrupt decrease or discontinuance of blood stream to the mind, prompting localized necrosis. The clinical administration of stroke is difficult and current medications must be regulated inside a constrained time window after the beginning of the stroke to give clinical advantage. Promising possibility for neuroprotective procedures incorporate preconditioning, mellow hypothermia, and the utilization of synthetic and organic mixes focusing on basic sub-atomic go betweens of neuronal demise and endurance.

The neuroprotective impact of SIRT1 was first revealed in ischemic preconditioning and the SIRT1 enacting compound resveratrol diminished neuronal damage of the hippocampus in worldwide cerebral ischemia in rodents. Expanded SIRT1 action was additionally demonstrated to be a typical instrument for the defensive impacts of preconditioning and resveratrol (Raval et al., 2006; Morris et al., 2011). Sirtinol, an inhibitor of SIRT1 movement, canceled the neuroprotection of preconditioning and resveratrol (Raval et al., 2006), showing that SIRT1 assumes a key job in interceding neuroprotection. This neuroprotective job is additionally bolstered by two ongoing investigations (Chong and Maiese, 2008; Della-Morte et al., 2009) indicating that SIRT1 actuation lessens ischemic neuronal wounds.

Another investigation demonstrated that, in essential neuronal culture, pretreatment with NAD+ pretreatment extraordinarily diminishes neuronal demise incited by oxygen-glucose hardship, an in vitro model of ischemia (Wang et al., 2008). SIRT1 is important for NAD+

67

neuroprotection, as NAD+ treatment upregulates SIRT1 articulation and movement, and SIRT1 knockdown lessens the assurance interceded by NAD+ (Wang et al., 2008). NAMPT overexpression decreases ischemic infarct, while NAMPT hindrance irritates ischemic wounds. The defensive impact of NAMPT is SIRT1-subordinate, as SIRT1 knockout hinders the security (Wang et al., 2011).

Regardless of the previously mentioned proof, debate exists over the defensive impact of SIRT1 against ischemia. In an examination with SIRT1 transgenic mice, where human SIRT1 was overexpressed heavily influenced by rodent neuron-specific enolase advertiser, no neuroprotection was seen against stroke as SIRT1 and wild-type mice exhibited practically vague infarct volumes and neurological insufficiency scores (Kakefuda et al., 2009). The error between this examination and the others was most likely because of the continued significant level of SIRT1, on the grounds that it might devour excessively or even exhaust NAD+, which could overstate neuronal damage (Wang et al., 2008; Kakefuda et al., 2009; Liu et al., 2009). Therefore, it is conceivable that NAD+ inadequacy bargained the neuroprotective impact of SIRT1. In another investigation, nicotinamide, an intensify that hinders SIRT1 activity, demonstrated neuroprotection against ischemic damage, inferring that SIRT1 may have an unfavorable impact against stroke (Chong et al., 2005). Be that as it may, this report may neglect different elements of nicotinamide, including that of antecedent for NAD+ amalgamation. Truth be told, a similar gathering later detailed that SIRT1 overexpression keeps neurons from apoptosis after oxidative pressure (Chong and Maiese, 2008).

SIRT1 in Clinical Practice

SIRT1-actuating mixes have not yet been demonstrated to be clinically valuable for the treatment of neurodegenerative illnesses. Preclinical investigations have been acted in different neurodegenerative malady models, in any case. The data acquired from such examinations could end up being significant for planning SIRT1-initiating particles that might be bound to be helpful clinically. The revelation of such atoms is getting progressively significant, considering the confinements of hereditary controls and the absence of unequivocal proof of specific SIRT1 initiation by model particles like resveratrol (Sauve, 2009).

A few levelheaded procedures dependent on the accessible protein structure and the synergist pathways have been intended to grow little particles that specifically enact sirtuins (Sauve, 2009). One technique includes planning resveratrol-like atoms, which has not yielded victories as the in vivo system of SIRT1 actuation isn't completely comprehended. Another methodology expects to expand the cell levels of NAD+ so as to initiate SIRT1 work. This methodology has the upside of tackling a characteristic metabolic pathway to improve SIRT1 capacities. In addition, normally happening metabolites present minimal danger of poisonous quality. The efficacies of operators that have been utilized to improve NAD+ are as yet faulty, notwithstanding, and NAD+ upgrade influences a large group of other physiological pathways, with the goal that the methodology isn't specific to SIRT1. A third technique as of now in the confirmation of-guideline arrange assigned nicotinamide derepression depends on countering the inhibitory impact of nicotinamide on sirtuins by planning particles that are opposing to nicotinamide. This methodology is still in its early stages and has not furnished mixes with wanted power, however is an appealing system to grow further. Subtleties of endeavors to find SIRT1-enacting particles have as of late been extensively surveyed by Blum et al. (2011).

Future Perspectives on SIRT1

Throughout the most recent decade, our comprehension of the science of sirtuins has immeasurably expanded from its unique portrayal as a NAD+-subordinate class III histone deacetylase that can control the lifespan of yeast. Specifically compelling is the revelation that SIRT1 deacetylates histones, yet additionally some outstanding transcriptional controllers, along these lines balancing a wide cluster of organic procedures. An energizing angle is that SIRT1 intercedes neuroprotection against both intense and ceaseless neurological infections. Significantly, SIRT1 movement is improved by little particle mixes; therefore, advancement of little atom activators could prompt novel treatments against neurological ailments. One of the wide defensive systems of SIRT1 is to stifle genome-wide quality interpretation by means of histone deacetylation. Besides, SIRT1 specifically smothers qualities associated with fat stockpiling, apoptosis, and aggravation. Adding to the multifaceted nature of

SIRT1-interceded cell endurance, SIRT1 specifically advances the translation of a lot of qualities identified with cell endurance, vitality digestion, and mitochondrial biogenesis. SIRT1 in this manner has multifaceted components with the ultimate objective to expand cell feasibility.

Albeit broadly contemplated, the natural elements of SIRT1 stay just in part portrayed. As for instrument of activity, there are a few significant questions. For instance, it isn't known how SIRT1 specifically builds translation of valuable qualities while it at the same time stifles widespread interpretation. It would hold any importance with decide if comparative instruments exist for qualities upregulated by SIRT1-interceded enactment of interpretation. Another issue is the incomprehensible impact of SIRT1. For instance, though SIRT1 straightforwardly smothers PPARγ transcriptional action legitimately (Picard et al., 2004), it likewise enacts PGC-1α (Nemoto et al., 2005; Rodgers et al., 2005), which could build the transcriptional exercises of PPARγ (Puigserver et al., 1998).

In spite of the fact that SIRT1 has been seen as neuroprotective in various investigations, it is obvious from the different obsessive systems manifested in neurodegenerative issue that the job of SIRT1 requires progressively nitty gritty examination. The accessibility of precious stone structures and definite unthinking examination are useful in finding SIRT1 modulators, however would be of constrained worth if they neglected to arrive at clinical preliminaries, hence accentuating the significance of creating hearty creature models for exploring atomic systems associated with SIRT1 actuation. Additionally, the potential negative impacts of SIRT1 actuation and vitality exhaustion need further examination in creature models. The clinical accomplishment of sirtuin initiating mixes (STACs) in neurodegenerative infections depends overwhelmingly on growing new procedures and planning particles dependent on the sirtuin science and sub-atomic pathways actuated by SIRT1. An ongoing report performed by Hubbard et al. (2013) exhibited that the specific hydrophobic motifs in SIRT1 substrates, for example, PGC-1α and FOXO3a encourage SIRT1 enactment by STACs, inferring that SIRT1 can be straightforwardly initiated through an allosteric instrument basic to synthetically assorted STACs. In rundown, there is no uncertainty that SIRT1 holds promising helpful potential for neurodegenerative issue.

SIRT3, Energy Metabolism and Aging

This segment outlines the investigations on the job of mitochondrial SIRT3 in vitality digestion and security against oxidative pressure and age-related brokenness (Figure 2).

SIRT3 and Mitochondria

Mitochondria are the powerhouse for ATP creation as well as the primary destinations where responsive oxygen species (ROS) are produced and the natural apoptotic flagging pathway is started (Salminen et al., 2008b). The elements of mitochondrial proteins are modified when they are deacetylated by NAD+-subordinate mitochondrial deacetylases, including SIRT3, SIRT4, and SIRT5. All mitochondrial sirtuins are available in the mitochondrial network (Howitz et al., 2003; Rogina and Helfand, 2004). Since mitochondria contain their very own DNA, translation factors, histone-like proteins, and protein union frameworks, mitochondrial sirtuins deacetylate a lot of focuses inside the mitochondria that are particular from those of atomic proteins (Tissenbaum and Guarente, 2001; Wood et al., 2004). Albeit exact unthinking data is as yet deficient with regards to, proof is rising to recommend that mitochondrial sirtuins ensure against oxidative pressure (Braunstein et al., 1993; Baur et al., 2006).

Among the mitochondrial sirtuins, SIRT3 capacities have been described in the best detail. Beginning investigations of SIRT3-insufficient mice showed that loss of SIRT3, yet not SIRT4 or SIRT5, prompted sensational protein hyperacetylation inside mitochondria, proposing that SIRT3 is the major mitochondrial deacetylase action (Dali-Youcef et al., 2007). In people, full-length SIRT3 is a 44-kD protein with a N-terminal mitochondrial focusing on succession that is an enzymatically inert in vitro. It is proteolytically prepared in mitochondria to a develop 28 kD chemically dynamic deacetylase (Onyango et al., 2002; Schwer et al., 2002). The principal mouse SIRT3 cDNA succession identified encoded a 28-kD protein coming up short on the N-terminal mitochondrial focusing on grouping (Yang et al., 2000). A few ongoing investigations have identified a more extended isoform of murine SIRT3 encoding a 37 kD protein, nonetheless, that can be brought into mitochondria and prepared into the develop 28 kD protein (Cooper et al., 2009; Jin et al., 2009; Bao et al., 2010; Yang et al., 2010). Regardless of whether a functioning portion of SIRT3 exists outside mitochondria and modifies extra-mitochondrial proteins stays dubious.

SIRT3 and Metabolic Homeostasis

Rising information have indicated that one significant capacity of SIRT3 is guideline of mitochondrial electron transport affix action to keep up vitality homeostasis. The primary vitality source in mitochondria is pyruvate, a result of glycolysis. On the other hand, mitochondria likewise consume unsaturated fats, amino acids, and acetic acid derivations when pyruvate is lacking. For unsaturated fat catabolism, long-chain acyl coenzyme A dehydrogenase (LCAD) is a key protein that separates unsaturated fats and produces acetyl-CoA, invigorating β-oxidation. In SIRT3 knockout mice, LCAD is hyperacetylated at Lys42, prompting diminishes in enzymatic action, β-oxidation, and ATP level (Hirschey et al., 2010). Strangely, these mice don't endure cold introduction during fasting (Hirschey et al., 2010). SIRT3 legitimately deacetylates LACD at Lys42 and builds LACD action (Hirschey et al., 2010). Also, SIRT3 may advance β-oxidation by means of numerous components, for example, by deacetylating other β-oxidation chemicals, including the short-chain L-3-hydroxyacyl-CoA dehydrogenase and the extremely long-chain acyl coenzyme A dehydrogenase (Hallows et al., 2011), encouraging mitochondrial adjustment to fuel changes.

Glucose is the significant vitality hotspot for cells. When its accessibility is restricted, nonetheless, elective fills become progressively significant for cell endurance. The initial step of glycolysis is the transformation of glucose to glucose-6-phosphate, a response catalyzed by hexokinases. It is accounted for that SIRT3 deacetylates cyclophilin D (Hafner et al., 2010; Shulga et al., 2010), which prompts the separation of hexokinase II and mitochondria, diminishes glucose digestion, and invigorates oxidative phosphorylation (Shulga et al., 2010).

Acetic acid derivation got from acidic corrosive and liquor is likewise utilized as a mitochondrial fuel, in spite of the fact that this just happens in outrageous conditions of supplement exhaustion. In the underlying advance acetic acid derivation is changed over to acetyl-CoA catalyzed by acetyl-CoA synthetases. Acetyl-CoA synthetase 2 is the mitochondrial type of the compound. SIRT3 deacetylates acetyl-CoA synthetase 2 and improves its movement, prompting expanded generation of acetyl-CoA (Hallows et al., 2006; Schwer et al., 2006). The acetyl-CoA from unsaturated fats and acetic acid derivations just as α-ketoglutarate from amino acids can enter the Krebs cycle. These two responses are upgraded by SIRT3 (Hallows et al., 2006; Schwer et al., 2006; Lombard et al., 2007; Schlicker et al., 2008). Furthermore, SIRT3 legitimately invigorates the Krebs cycle. The third step of the cycle is the change of 6-carbon isocitrate to 5-carbon α-ketoglutarate, a procedure catalyzed by isocitrate dehydrogenase 2 (IDH2). An ongoing report shows that SIRT3 legitimately deacetylates this dehydrogenase to build its movement (Someya et al., 2010).

NADH dehydrogenase 1 alpha subcomplex subunit 9 (NDUFA9) is a chemical of mitochondrial complex I that is acetylated at Lys370 (Kim et al., 2006). SIRT3 physically interfaces with NDUFA9 and deacetylates it. SIRT3 knockout improves its acetylation and decreases the movement of complex I (Ahn et al., 2008), showing that SIRT3 is a positive controller of complex I. Complex II, otherwise called succinate dehydrogenase, is made out of four subunits, including the flavoprotein succinate dehydrogenase subunit A (SdhA). In SIRT3 knockout mice, SdhA is hyperacetylated at a few lysine deposits, and shows diminished action of complex II (Cimen et al., 2010). SIRT3 overexpression switches the acetylation of SdhA and builds complex II action (Cimen et al., 2010), showing that SdhA is a SIRT3 substrate, and that SIRT3 is likewise a positive controller of complex II.

SIRT3 is likewise answered to tie the alpha subunit 1 of the F1 molecule of ATP synthase (Law et al., 2009), yet the capacity is hazy. Taken together, these outcomes propose that SIRT3 advances ATP age through improving activity of a few catalysts associated with vitality digestion. Further supporting this job, SIRT3-knockout mice show generous acetylation of mitochondrial proteins, and have decreased ATP levels at gauge and during cell stress (Ahn et al., 2008).

Mitochondria are additionally the significant destinations for the age of the ROS, superoxide, and furthermore where the superoxide is dismuted by mitochondrial MnSOD. Late reports show that SIRT3 deacetylates MnSOD at Lys122 and builds its movement, lessening oxidative and radiation worry in mice (Qiu et al., 2010; Tao et al., 2010). Overexpression of SIRT3 shields HEK293 from oxidative pressure and forestalls age-related cochlear cell passing in mice (Someya et al., 2010). In general, this proposes hostile to oxidative and neuroprotective jobs of SIRT3. New information propose that the SIRT3 deacetylase assumes a key job in supporting mitochondrial against oxidant protections during CR (Qiu et al., 2010; Someya et al., 2010).

In future examinations, it will bear some significance with characterize the instrument whereby acetylation of electron transport chain subunits influences age of ATP. It is additionally critical to explain why it may be attractive under some physiologic conditions to downregulate electron transport chain movement by expanded acetylation. As an additional wrinkle, SIRT3 contrarily manages interpretation inside mitochondria by deacetylating the ribosomal protein MRPL10, a capacity proposed to decrease breath (Yang et al., 2010).

SIRT3 levels are expanded in fat tissue, skeletal muscle, and liver during CR (Shi et al., 2005; Palacios et al., 2009; Schwer et al., 2009; Hirschey et al., 2010), and then again decrease because of high-fat encouraging (Palacios et al., 2009; Bao et al., 2010; Kendrick et al., 2011). These articulation information recommend that SIRT3 may assume a job in the reaction to metabolic homeostasis. In warm blooded creatures, two free examinations demonstrated that SIRT3 cooperates with and deacetylates acetyl-CoA synthetase 2 (AceCS2) at the dynamic site lysine to advance AceCS2 movement (Hallows et al., 2006; Schwer et al., 2006). Starved conditions, most of acetyl-CoA is created through digestion of pyruvate by Pyruvate dehydrogenase complex (PDC) and by unsaturated fat β-oxidation, to a great extent bypassing the requirement for AceCS2. In such manner, investigations of AceCS2-lacking mice uncovered that AceCS2 is specifically required for metabolic homeostasis when the mice are encouraged a low starch/high fat diet (LC/HFD); AceCS2-inadequate creatures are basically ordinary on a chow diet however show poor weight gain, hypothermia, hypoglycemia, and debilitated endurance on a LC/HFD (Sakakibara et al., 2009). Apparently the job of SIRT3 in directing AceCS2 could likewise be significant during fasting, when acetic acid derivation can be utilized as a wellspring of vitality in extrahepatic tissues (Hirschey et al., 2010). Without a doubt, SIRT3 has as of late been appeared to deacetylate and actuate 3-hydroxy-3-methylglutaryl-CoA synthase 2 (HMGCS2), a mitochondrial compound that changes over acetyl-CoA into ketone bodies (acetoacetate, β-hydroxybutyrate, and CH3)2CO) in the liver under fasting conditions, which can thusly be utilized as a wellspring of vitality in specific tissues including the mind (Shimazu et al., 2010). SIRT3-lacking mice can't deliver ordinary degrees of ketone bodies after fasting.

SIRT, Lifespan and Age-Associated Phenotypes

The job of SIRT3 in maturing is of significant intrigue since it seems to stifle ROS, one of the makes contributing the way toward maturing.

Notwithstanding explaining its jobs in controlling specific biochemical pathways in mitochondria, there is extraordinary enthusiasm for testing whether SIRT3 may tweak age-related phenotypes, or for sure lifespan itself. In such manner, a few investigations have connected polymorphisms in the SIRT3 genomic locus to human life span, despite the fact that others have neglected to show this affiliation (Rose et al., 2003; Bellizzi et al., 2005, 2007; Lescai et al., 2009). A polymorphism related with diminished SIRT3 mRNA articulation was available in partners of youthful however not elderly people men, recommending that decreased SIRT3 articulation might be inconvenient to endurance in mature age (Bellizzi et al., 2005, 2009). In inactive people, SIRT3 protein articulation declined with age in skeletal muscle mitochondria, attending with a decrease in respiratory capacity (Lanza et al., 2008).

Age-related hearing loss (ARHL) is a typical issue in the older, happening optional to cell loss and other degenerative changes in the cochlea. A rich examination has immovably settled a job for SIRT3 in forestalling ARHL (Someya et al., 2010). One component by which SIRT3 intercedes this impact is by deacetylation of IDH2 (Schlicker et al., 2008; Someya et al., 2010), which changes over isocitrate to α-ketoglutarate corresponding with decrease of NADP+. NADPH thus permits recovery of decreased glutathione to advance mitochondrial oxidative protection. In light of CR, wild-type mice, however not SIRT3-insufficient creatures, show expanded NADPH levels, expanded diminished glutathione in mitochondria, and diminished

DNA harm in the cochlea and in different tissues. In tissue culture cells, overexpression of SIRT3 or IDH2 ensures against oxidative pressure actuated cell demise, and the two proteins together have a synergistic genius endurance impact. These outcomes don't decide out the likelihood that SIRT3 may modify different substrates notwithstanding IDH2 to forestall AHRL during CR. Essentially, Qiu et al. (2010) revealed that SIRT3-insufficient mice neglect to stifle ROS levels and macromolecular harm during CR. They find that SIRT3 legitimately deacetylates SOD2 to expand its action during CR, while SIRT3-insufficient mice don't show SOD2 deacetylation because of this diet (Qiu et al., 2010). By and large, these papers point to urgent job for SIRT3 in stifling oxidative harm and its negative continuation during CR. It is not yet clear how SIRT3, or the other mitochondrial sirtuins, might influence different phenotypes of maturing as well as impacts of CR. The decrease of serum insulin and triglycerides that regularly happens during CR isn't seen in SIRT3-lacking mice (Someya et al., 2010), suggesting that SIRT3 plays extra, uncharacterized jobs in the adjustment to this dietary routine. An ongoing report shows that upregulation of SIRT3 undoubtedly turns around maturing related degeneration in hematopoietic immature microorganisms (Brown et al., 2013), and SIRT3 may advance organismal life span by keeping up the uprightness of tissue-specific foundational microorganisms.

SIRT3 and Mitochondrial Protein Acetylation: Unresolved Questions

Acetylation of mitochondrial proteins assumes a significant job in controlling elements of this organelle. Regardless of the fast advancement around there, there are as yet numerous extraordinary inquiries remain that will no uncertainty give productive roads to explore for quite a long time to come. Specifically, how mitochondrial proteins are acetylated in any case is as of now obscure. The personality of putative mitochondrial acetyltransferases stays slippery; identification of such proteins would speak to a significant advance forward in this field. Then again, or notwithstanding enzymatic acetylation inside mitochondria, mitochondrial proteins could on a fundamental level be acetylated outside this organelle, before or accompanying with mitochondrial import or even be acetylated non-enzymatically. These last models would not allow fast cycles of acetylation/deacetylation of mitochondrial proteins to manage target protein work in light of fluctuated ecological difficulties. Rather, after deacetylation, reclamation of acetylation status would require new protein combination. Such models could be recognized through heartbeat pursue tests evaluating acetylation of recently orchestrated mitochondrial proteins before and after mitochondrial import.

Thus, how SIRT3 action is controlled in the mitochondria is not completely comprehended. SIRT3 requires NAD+, and therefore mitochondrial NAD+ levels assume a fundamentally significant job in administering mitochondrial SIRT3 work. Expanded NADH age from NAD+ that happens with HFD and prompts diminished SIRT3 capacity may clarify the expanded worldwide mitochondrial protein acetylation saw during this diet, as could build levels of acetyl-CoA, the substrate for acetyltransferases (Kendrick et al., 2011). This general expanded acetylation may speak to the net impact of expanded acetyltransferase action superimposed upon raised SIRT3 work; on the other hand, some protein species hyperacetylated during CR or different conditions may not be substrates for mitochondrial SIRT3. The movement of SIRT3 and other mitochondrial sirtuins may be impacted by different conditions notwithstanding NAD+ levels, for example, post-translational modification or connections with administrative proteins.

Further Perspectives

In the previous decade, the capacity of mammalian sirtuins has been researched in more prominent detail than at any other time, and we currently have a vastly improved sub-atomic comprehension of the various jobs this special group of compounds plays in apparently every natural procedure. There is little uncertainty that sirtuins have risen as basic modulators of metabolic versatile reactions, and their exercises have been connected to metabolic anomalies just as age-related neurodegeneration. However, key inquiries will keep agents occupied in the coming years. We despite everything have poor comprehension of the sub-atomic instruments managing articulation and movement of the sirtuins, and of the exact upgrades that direct these proteins, and whether the exercises of different sirtuins are controlled in a planned manner. As such, is there cross-talk between sirtuins? Will future examinations concrete the contention that sirtuins are, to be sure, basic modulators of lifespan? This survey has concentrated on SIRT1 and SIRT3. Indeed, even less is thought about different sirtuins. Further examination concerning the objectives and elements of this novel group of sirtuins will help grow new procedures for assurance against and recuperation from normal maturing related neurological illnesses and advance effective maturing.

Irreconcilable circumstance Statement

The creator pronounces that the examination was led without any business or monetary connections that could be understood as a potential irreconcilable circumstance.

PROS AND CONS OF SIRTFOOD DIET

The Sirtfood diet has become the 'new' prevailing fashion of 2016 and has picked up acknowledgment from famous people like TV gourmet expert Lorraine Pascale. It is broadly known for permitting you to have dim chocolate and red wine and still get in shape, sounds somewhat insane right? If you're similar to me and possess a solid incredulity about the most recent diet slants, we should right away, discover more and consider The Pros and Cons of the Sirtfood Diet!

Stars:

The 'sirt nourishments' as far as anyone knows enact the sirtuin in your body which is a sort of protein that assists with shielding your cells from kicking the bucket and creating sicknesses, just as managing your digestion

It depends on an investigation of 40 exercise center goers who each lost by and large 7lb in multi week without losing bulk

You can have moderate measures of dull chocolate and wine all the time without feeling remorseful!

It contains nourishments that are commonly sound and nutritious, for example, buckwheat, blueberries, pecans and green tea

It's intended to be long haul and keep you sound for life just as hindering the maturing procedure

Cons:

For the principal week there is a calorie limitation that will no uncertainty power a great many people to get more fit, paying little heed to what nourishment is devoured. This implies it might be because of the calorie limitation itself that the members shed pounds. For the initial three days you just expend 1,000 calories per day and the accompanying four days are comprised of 1,500 calories for each day

Radically limiting your calorie admission can be risky if your body isn't utilized to it and can cause you to feel dormant

There isn't sufficient proof that it finishes on its guarantees, particularly the accelerating of your digestion. An investigation on 40 individuals isn't sufficiently huge to state that it will work as a solid method to get in shape

You can just have nourishments on the sirtfood rundown, for example, 'sirt juices', rocket, soy, green tea and pecans

Because of the above mentioned, there's less accentuation on getting an assortment of nourishments into your diet so as to look and feel extraordinary. For instance eating a rainbow of foods grown from the ground each day guarantees you get a scope of nutrients and minerals into your diet.

Why Everyone Is Talking About the Sirtfood Diet?

"Sirtfood" seems like something created by outsiders, brought to earth for human utilization with expectations of picking up mind control and global control. In reality, sirtfoods are just nourishments high in sirtuins. Uh, come back once more? Sirtuins are a sort of protein that reviews on natural product flies and mice have demonstrated control digestion, increment bulk, and consume fat.

The Sirtfood Diet book was first distributed in the U.K. in 2016. In any case, the U.S. arrival of the book, coming this March, has started greater interest about the arrangement. The diet started getting publicity when Adele debuted her slimmer figure at the Billboard Music Awards last May. Her mentor, Pete Geracimo, is an enormous devotee of the diet and says the vocalist shed 30 pounds from following a sirtfood diet. (Here, Adele gets genuine about getting sound.)

According to the book, this arrangement can assist you with consuming fat and lift your vitality, preparing your body for long haul weight-loss achievement and a more drawn out, more advantageous, illness free life. All that while drinking red wine. Sounds like practically the ideal diet, isn't that so? All things considered, before you consume your reserve funds loading up on sirtuins-filled fixings, read the upsides and downsides.

How can it work?

At its center, the way to getting more fit is quite straightforward: Create a calorie shortage either by expanding your calorie consume workouts or diminishing your caloric admission. Yet, imagine a scenario in which you could avoid the dieting and rather enact a "thin quality" without the requirement for exceptional calorie limitation. This is the reason of The Sirtfood Diet, composed by sustenance specialists Aidan Goggins and Glen Matten. The best approach to do it, they contend, is sirtfoods.

Sirtfoods are wealthy in supplements that actuate a supposed "thin quality" called sirtuin. According to Goggins and Matten, the "thin quality" is initiated when a lack of vitality is made after you limit calories. Sirtuins got intriguing to the nourishment world in 2003 when specialists found that resveratrol, a compound found in red wine, had a similar impact on life length as calorie limitation yet it was accomplished without lessening admission. (Discover the complete truth about wine and its medical advantages.)

In the 2015 pilot study (led by Goggins and Matten) testing the viability of sirtuins, the 39 members lost a normal of seven pounds in seven days. Those outcomes sound great, however it's imperative to understand this is a little example size concentrated over a brief timeframe. Weight-loss specialists additionally have their questions about the grand guarantees. "The cases made are theoretical and extrapolate from examines which were for the most part centered around straightforward life forms (like yeast) at the cell level. What occurs at the cell level doesn't really mean what occurs in the human body at the large scale level," says Adrienne Youdim, M.D., the executive of the Center for Weight Loss and Nutrition in Beverly Hills, CA. (Here, look at the best and most noticeably awful diets to follow this year.)

What nourishments are high in sirtuins?

The book contains a rundown of the main 20 nourishments that are high in sirtuins, which sounds more like a drifting nourishment list than another, advanced diet. Models include: arugula, chilies, espresso, green tea, Medjool dates, red wine, turmeric, pecans, and the wellbeing cognizant top choice kale. Dr. Youdim takes note of that while the nourishments being advanced are solid, they won't really advance weight loss all alone.

What does the diet involve?

The diet is executed in two stages. Stage one endures three days and limits calories to 1,000 every day, comprising of three green juices and one sirtfood-endorsed feast. Stage two keeps going four days and raises the day by day apportioning to 1,500 calories for every day with two green juices and two dinners.

After these stages, there is a support plan that isn't centered around calories yet rather on reasonable parts, well-adjusted dinners, and topping off on principally sirtfoods. The 14-day upkeep plan highlights three dinners, one green juice, and a couple sirtfood nibble snacks. Devotees are additionally urged to finish 30 minutes of movement five days per week-per government suggestions however it isn't the fundamental focal point of the arrangement.

What are the advantages?

You will get thinner if you follow this diet intently. "Regardless of whether you're eating 1,000 calories of tacos, 1,000 calories of kale, or 1,000 calories of snickerdoodles, you will get more fit at 1,000 calories!" says Dr. Youdim. Yet, she likewise calls attention to that you can have accomplishment with an increasingly sensible calorie limitation. The run of the mill day by day caloric admission of somebody not on a diet is 2,000 to 2,200, so diminishing to 1,500 is as yet confining and would be a successful weight-loss methodology for most, she says.

Are there any precautionary measures?

This arrangement is severe with little squirm room or substitutions, and weight loss must be kept up if the low caloric admission is additionally kept up, making it difficult to hold fast to long haul. That implies any weight you lost in the initial seven days is probably going to be recovered after you finish, says Dr. Youdin. Her fundamental concern? "Restricting protein consumption with juices will bring about a loss of bulk. Losing muscle is synonymous with dropping your metabolic rate or 'digestion,' making weight upkeep progressively difficult," she says.

Last Thoughts

By and large, Dr. Youdim would not suggest this diet. There are different ways that you can lessen calorie admission without being so prohibitive in the nourishments that you eat. All things considered, the diet isn't really "unfortunate" so she wouldn't really alert against it if a patient discovered achievement.

If you do follow this arrangement, make certain to eat a lot of protein and shift the nourishments you eat to forestall nutrient insufficiencies. Our take? The diet is extraordinarily exacting and its viability has not been enough demonstrated. You're greatly improved off building up a lifestyle of eating an assortment of entire nourishments in the extents that suit your individual needs.

The Sirtfood diet has been on the scene for a couple of years however enthusiasm for the eating plan is recharged thanks its detailed job in Adele's ongoing weight loss.

Here's all that you have to think about the Sirtfood diet, from what it includes to whether it truly works.

What is the Sirtfood diet?

The Sirtfood diet was created by UK nutritionists Aidan Goggins and Glen Matten, who distributed a top rated book on the point in 2016. It vows to lessen irritation, lengthen your life range, turn on your "thin quality" and assist you with shedding seven pounds (three kilograms) in seven days. It asserts that eating specific nourishments will interface with a gathering of proteins found in the body called sirtuins (SIRTs), which are engaged with a wide scope of cell forms including digestion, maturing and circadian cadence.

Beside expending a scope of "sirtfoods" the diet includes phases of calorie limitation, which is likewise said to enable the body to create more sirtuins. During the initial three says calorie admission is restricted to 1,000 every day, sourced from three green juices and sirtfood-rich dinner. For the remainder of the week, calorie admission is helped to 1,500 every day from two juices and two dinners. The subsequent stage keeps going 14 days and prompts three adjusted sirtfood rich suppers daily alongside one sirtfood green juice. Long haul its advocates suggest eating suppers with however many Sirtfoods as could reasonably be expected.

What nourishments would you be able to eat on the Sirtfood diet?

Kale

Red wine

Strawberries

Onions

Soy

Parsley

Additional virgin olive oil

Dull chocolate (85% cocoa)

Matcha green tea

Buckwheat

Turmeric

Pecans

Rocket

10,000 foot stew

Lovage

Medjool dates

Red chicory

Blueberries

Tricks

Espresso

You can get a total rundown of sirtfoods suggested on the diet inside the book.

What are the medical advantages of the Sirtfood diet? Would it be able to assist you with getting in shape?

Nutritionist Rick Hay discloses to Women's Health that a few upsides of eating a lot of Sirtfoods is an expansion fiber admission and the considerable measure of micronutrients called polyphenols can improve heart wellbeing. Be that as it may, the cons exceed the geniuses.

"While limiting your calories and certain nutrition types for the most part prompts weight loss for the time being," nutritionist Rick Hay reveals to Women's Health. "The Sirtfood diet is very prohibitive – it centers around calorie checking and expects you to remove significant nutrition types. You will likewise need to scale back your segments, particularly in week one. Another drawback is the way that the diet may need fundamental supplements, for example, calcium and iron."

What does the science state?

Research on mice, yeast and human undifferentiated organisms has inspected the job that sirtuins play in broadening life range however these can't really be extrapolated to people. When it goes to the Sirtfood diet, there's been no long haul human investigations on in the case of expending Sirtfoods have any medical advantages or weight loss results.

What are the threats of the Sirtfood diet?

"If you're not utilized confining your nourishment consumption during the day, you may likewise encounter sickness, unsteadiness, difficulty concentrating, exhaustion, and migraines," Hay cautions. "If you've at any point endured with a dietary problem or had a confused association with eating before, it's ideal to abstain from jumping on the Sirtfood Diet wagon – simply fuse a greater amount of Sirtfoods into your diet and cut out prepared nourishments and sugar and exercise a few times each week."

Rather than empowering starvation and blame about calorie consumption, The Sirtfood Diet is tied in with utilizing 'wonderfoods' to turbocharge your body to build weight loss, however to improve your wellbeing by and large in the long haul.

Not advocated by big names as a prevailing fashion diet, rather The SirtFood Diet has been prescribed by sports characters, for example, British fighter David Haye, Olympic gold medalist Ben Ainslie and English ruby player James Haskell who all depend on their bodies performing at their best.

Also, if that wasn't sufficient to persuade you to check out it, all things considered individuals had the option to get in shape quick – seven pounds (3.2kg) in just seven days on the Sirtfood Diet, actually.

Indeed, you read that effectively, that is a large portion of a stone in only multi week!

We're tuning in.

What is The Sirtfood Diet?

The organizers of The Sirtfood Diet are Aidan Goggins and Glen Matte, both prepared nutritionists who have figured out how to saddle the intensity of 'Sirtfood' science to make a progressive diet.

The science behind the diet is altogether based around these Sirtfoods, which are a gathering of as of late found regular plant nourishments high in a substance compound known as 'sirtuin' activators.

These sirtuin activators are a sort of protein, which switch on the supposed 'thin quality' pathways in the body.

These thin pathways are similar ones all the more regularly initiated by fasting and exercise and help the body to consume fat, to build bulk and improve your wellbeing.

Nations where individuals as of now expend countless Sirtfoods as a component of their customary diet, including Japan and Italy, are both routinely positioned among the most beneficial nations on the planet.

Aidan and Glen have quite recently discharged their book; The Sirtfood Diet – the progressive arrangement for wellbeing and weight loss.

How can it work?

Sirtfoods animate sirtuin qualities, which are said to impact the body's capacity to consume fat and lift the metabolic framework.

The Sirtfood diet depends on two phases;

Stage one is a serious seven-day program intended to launch your exceptional weight loss.

Then stage two is tied in with increasing the amount of Sirtfood-rich produce in your ordinary dinners to keep up weight loss.

Dissimilar to numerous other present moment yo-yo diets, the Sirtfood plan remembers suppers and guidance for how to keep off the weight you lose in the main week by proceeding to incorporate Sirtfoods as a feature of a sound and adjusted diet.

What does a commonplace day resemble?

Stage One

For the initial three days dieters drink two green squeezes a day – including kale, celery, rocket, parsley, lemon and green tea – and eat one feast.

For instance, the dinner can be something like turkey escalope with savvy, chicken and kale curry and prawn pan sear with buckwheat noodles or sesame-coated tofu if you're veggie lover. All made up of high Sirtfood fixings.

You can likewise have 15-20g of dim chocolate after your feast if you have a sweet tooth.

For the second 50% of your first week, you can have two juices and two suppers every day, with comparable fixings to the initial three days.

Stage Two

After the underlying phase of fasting the center shifts to eating 'ordinarily' once more, however increasing your admission of the sound Sirtfoods. Continue perusing for Aidan and Glen's first class Sirtfood fixings!

Who is it useful for?

In spite of the fact that the underlying phase of squeezing and fasting just appears to be useful for the individuals who should shift a couple of pounds rapidly, the general frame of mind of the Sirtfood diet is to incorporate more beneficial nourishments into your diet to build your prosperity and lift your resistant framework after some time.

So while the initial seven days appear to be no-nonsense, the more drawn out term plan works for everybody.

By concentrating on bringing Sirtfood rich fixings into your ordinary suppers you can proceed with the fat consuming while making the most of your customary top choices.

Model Jodie Kidd says; 'Individuals continue asking me my mystery to looking incredible. The appropriate response is Aidan and Glen's Sirtfood diet. Since tailing it, I feel relentless.'

Lorraine Pascale, TV moderator, said; 'A non-faddy diet that offers mind blowing medical advantages and weight loss. Aidan and Glen show how everybody can receive the rewards of the Sirtfood diet through eating delightful nourishment. I'm an immense fan!'

Ben Ainslie says; 'I'm more advantageous, progressively alert, and in top physical condition. Sirtfoods are key for me arriving at new tops in execution to confront the up and coming difficulties.'

It isn't prescribed for pregnant ladies or those attempting to imagine.

What are the professionals?

The greatest expert is that red wine, dim chocolate and espresso are effectively supported on this diet – and that isn't something you often hear!

The intensifies that make up our preferred treats are rich in sirtuin activators. Despite the fact that obviously drinking a kale smoothie followed by an entire bar of Green and Blacks won't see you dropping the pounds. Everything with some restraint.

Aiden and Glen state that members seldom feel hungry – which implies it's useful for any individual who can't overcome one day of an ordinary wash down without feeling like they are going to black out except if they eat a Big Mac right away.

What are the cons?

The primary seven day stretch of the arrangement is truly in-your-face. Days one to three are generally escalated with your calorie admission restricted to 1000 – consolidated of three juices and one dinner.

Days four to seven are somewhat more indulgent with a calorie limit of 1,500 calories for each day.

Aidan and Glen express that so as to battle the fasting time frame, don't concentrate on how much weight you are losing, rather take a gander at the wellbeing sway on your tone and how your garments fit, also how brilliant your skin will look.

Video of the Week

They encourage fasters to spread the juices out for the duration of the day instead of having them excessively near one another. Expend the juices in any event an hour or two before and after dinners and don't eat any later than seven PM.

SIRTFOOD RECIPES

SIRTFOOD GREEN JUICE

Fixings:

2 enormous bunches (75g) kale

an enormous bunch (30g) rocket

a little bunch (5g) level leaf parsley

a little bunch (5g) lovage leaves (discretionary)

2–3 enormous stalks (150g) green celery, including its leaves

½ medium green apple

juice of ½ lemon

½ level tsp matcha green tea

INSTRUCTIONS:

Blend the greens (kale, rocket, parsley and lovage, if utilizing) together, then squeeze them. We discover juicers can truly differ in their effectiveness at squeezing verdant vegetables and you may need to re-squeeze the remainders before proceeding onward to different fixings. The objective is to wind up with about 50ml of juice from the greens.

Presently squeeze the celery and apple.

You can strip the lemon and put it through the juicer also, however we think that it's a lot simpler to just crush the lemon by hand into the juice. By this stage, you ought to have around 250ml of juice altogether, maybe somewhat more.

It is just when the juice is made and prepared to serve that you include the matcha green tea. Pour a modest quantity of the juice into a glass, then include the matcha and mix energetically with a fork or teaspoon. We just use matcha in the initial two beverages of the day as it contains moderate measures of caffeine (a similar substance as a typical cup of tea). For individuals not accustomed to it, it might keep them conscious if alcoholic late.

Once the matcha is broken up include the rest of the juice. Give it a last mix, then your juice is prepared to drink. Don't hesitate to top up with plain water, according to taste.

ASIAN KING PRAWN STIR-FRY WITH BUCKWHEAT NOODLES

Fixings:

150g shelled crude ruler prawns, deveined

2 tsp tamari (you can utilize soy sauce if you are not maintaining a strategic distance from gluten)

2 tsp additional virgin olive oil

75g soba (buckwheat noodles)

1 garlic clove, finely slashed

1 superior stew, finely slashed

1 tsp finely slashed new ginger

20g red onions, cut

40g celery, cut and cut

75g green beans, slashed

50g kale, generally slashed

100ml chicken stock

5g lovage or celery leaves

INSTRUCTIONS:

Warmth a skillet over a high warmth, then cook the prawns in 1 teaspoon of the tamari and 1 teaspoon of the oil for 2–3 minutes. Move the prawns to a plate. Wipe the work out with kitchen paper, as you're going to utilize it once more.

Cook the noodles in bubbling water for 5–8 minutes or as coordinated on the bundle. Channel and put in a safe spot.

Then, fry the garlic, stew and ginger, red onion, celery, beans and kale in the rest of the oil over a medium–high warmth for 2–3 minutes. Add the stock and bring to the bubble, then stew for a moment or two, until the vegetables are cooked yet at the same time crunchy.

Include the prawns, noodles and lovage/celery leaves to the dish, take back to the bubble then expel from the warmth and serve.

SALMON SIRT SUPER SALAD

Fixings:

50g rocket

50g chicory leaves

100g smoked salmon cuts

80g avocado, stripped, stoned and cut

40g celery, cut

20g red onion, cut

15g pecans, hacked

1 tbsp tricks

1 huge Medjool date, hollowed and slashed

1 tbsp additional virgin olive oil

juice of ¼ lemon

10g parsley, hacked

10g lovage or celery leaves, hacked

Directions:

Spot the serving of mixed greens leaves on a plate or in an enormous bowl. Combine all the rest of the fixings and serve over the leaves.

SIRTFOOD CHICKEN AND KALE CURRY

The turmeric in this dish includes a dazzling natural flavor. Tumeric and Kale are Sirtfoods and according to scientists, these extraordinary nourishments work by enacting specific proteins in the body called sirtuins. Sirtuins are accepted to shield cells in the body from biting the dust when they are under pressure and are thought to manage irritation, digestion and the maturing procedure. Analysts additionally accept sirtuins impact the body's capacity to consume fat and lift digestion.

Fixings

400 g Skinless and boneless chicken thighs

1 tbsp olive oil

2 tbsp ground tumeric

2 red onions, diced

3 garlic cloves, squashed

2 winged creatures eye bean stew finely cleaved

1 tbsp crisply cleaved ginger

1 tbsp curry powder

2 cardammon cases

1 tin cleaved tomatoes

200 ml tinned coconut milk, light

1 chicken stock pot

500 ml bubbling water

175 g tinned cleaved tomatoes

Chicken and kale curry photograph

Guidelines

Spot the chicken in a non-metalic bowl and include 1 tsp of the oil and 1 tbsp of the turmeric. Blend well and permit to marinate for 30 minutes. Be cautious when marinating as turmeric will recolor your fingers so mix with a spoon!

Then fry the chicken over a medium warmth for 4-5 minutes until sautéed all finished and cooked through. Expel from the dish and put in a safe spot.

Warmth the rest of the oil on a medium warmth and fry the onion, bean stew, garlic and ginger for 10 minutes until delicate. (Open the windows, it'll be very powerful!)

Include the curry powder and another tablespoon of the turmeric and cook for 1-2 minutes.

Include the tomatoes, stock, coconut milk and cardamom cases. Leave to stew for 30 minutes.

When the sauce has diminished a little include the chicken back in followed by the kale. Cook until the chicken has warmed through and the kale is delicate.

Present with buckwheat or rice. If utilizing buckwheat stew it for somewhat less time than prescribed on the parcel or you'll get a wet wreckage, it needs to hold a touch of nibble to it.

Trimming with cleaved coriander before serving.

SIRTFOOD GREEN JUICE

I'm on a diet. I don't ordinarily diet however my weight has expanded higher than any time in recent memory in the past couple months and I concluded it was the ideal opportunity for a change. Since the time I got T1D, I've thought that it was' significantly harder to get in shape. Insulin = Fat stockpiling and since I have to infuse insulin to live, it's a dilemma truly. In any case, since I can't take care of the entire insulin thing, I can take care of my diet. I as of now eat about 80% sound at any rate, heaps of natural products and vegetables (zucchini is my top choice) however as of recently I surmise I hadn't understood what amount nibbling I was doing... Since moving to London, I surmise there's only a mess more to nibble on and I mean there's much more garbage to eat. Join that with an excess of vino and the pounds included rapidly. Additional weight isn't actually useful when beginning to prepare for a long distance race either... particularly when it goes to my bionic foot. More weight implies more power and I need my foot to remain decent and solid and run in June with no wounds!

SIRTFOOD DIET

Since I improve if I have an arrangement, I realized I required one to follow to remain on track, I began investigating one that would work for me. I definitely realized Whole 30 wouldn't work so this end of the week when I read an article this end of the week about The Sirtfood Diet, I was interested. The Sirtfood Diet by Aidan Goggins and Glen Matten, records espresso, chocolate and red wine among it's solid alternatives. (sounds great as of now). Aidan, a pharmacologist and Glen, who holds a Masters certificate in dietary drug, met in 2012 when they distributed an investigate of the enhancement business – The Health Delusion (I'm perusing it next) in which they uncovered how a great many us are taking nutrient pills we don't really require and now and again are can be emphatically unfortunate since they give a lot higher measurements of supplements than are found in our nourishment. Also, as of late the pair began exploring sirtuins. So what precisely are sirtuins and how are they going to assist me with getting in shape... .

Sirtuins are a class of protein found in living things that are associated with metabolic procedures. 'Sirtfoods' are high in sirtuin activators, and copy the impacts of fasting and exercise by consuming fat, expanding muscle and fighting off ailment. (sounds incredible) According to Aidan and Glen, the writers of The Sirtfood Diet book (out today and just £8.00), loading up on sirtuin-rich nourishments, for example, kale, green tea and apples can animate the 'inside scoop' quality pathways and assist you with losing fat rapidly.

The main ten Sirtfoods are:

Green tea, Dark chocolate, Turmeric, Kale, Blueberries, Parsley, Capers, Citrus natural products, Apples, Red wine

Sirt-Nourishments Assortment

The arrangement appeared to be sufficiently simple – for the first 3 days drink 3 SIRT juices (formula underneath) 3 times each day then have a Sirtfood supper. Then, in days 4-7 beverage 2 SIRT juices daily and eat 2 Sirtfood dinners. The book expressed that nearly everybody who took an interest in the arrangement lost in any event 7 pounds in 7 days. WOWSERS. I'm as of now a juice convert with the goal that part was secured and since you're permitted espresso, red wine and dim chocolate (in little amounts) it seemed like an arrangement I could get behind.

Since the book didn't turn out until today, I utilized the plans in the book to kick me off and speculated on what little quanities implied, here's my week up until this point... My mornings have all been the equivalent, wake up and drink a tea and some lemon water. Somewhat later have a coffee and afterward attempt and hold up till 10am until I drink my first squeeze and when I do eat a modest piece of protein with it (not on plan) to slow the ingestion of sugar from the juice (because of my T1D).

Monday – Loads of water, tea, coffee, 1 mug of SIRT juice 3 X daily, (minor piece of protein included 1 hard bubbled egg white, 1 3oz part of chicken and a bunch of shelled edamame), a little square of 85% dull chocolate and a sirtfood supper – 100% Buckwheat noodles with veggies and chicken (formula one week from now)

Buckwheat Noodles Sirt Dinner

I was wanting a bite however not on the grounds that I was ravenous... in light of the fact that I was so used to eating throughout the day. NO appetite torments and after supper I was full to the gills. First time attempting buckwheat pasta and I cherished it... so did the hubby (he was stunned).

Tuesday – Loads of water, tea, coffee, 1 mug of SIRT juice 3 X daily, (3 minor bits of protein included 2 hard bubbled egg white and 1 3oz bit of chicken), a little square (10g) of 85% Lindt dim chocolate and a sirtfood supper – Spiced cauliflower couscous with escapades, parsley and chicken (could go veggie lover or use shrimp) – formula one week from now

No craving agonies and couldn't complete juice #3, just drank half. When supper moves around, the arrangement says to eat after 7:30pm, I was eager. The supper was another grand slam formula (even the hubby adored it) and I completed with a full stomach. Rested soundly and wok up feeling superior to anything I had in months!

Wednesday – 1L water, tea, 1 cup SIRT juice 2 x daily, (2 little bits of protein included 1 hard bubbled egg white and 1 3oz part of chicken), square of dim chocolate, 6oz glass of red wine*, sirtfood supper and another little square of dull chocolate before bed.

By and by, zero appetite torments. Truth be told, I was so full I was unable to try and drink my third squeeze of the day – rather I decided on an early supper and bed by 9:30 rather than the typical 11pm (since I had an early morning today). For supper I made my own sirtfood feast and once more, it was delightful. I'm beginning to think this arrangement was made for me…

Today – Thursday – I chose to step on the scale. I realized I was feeling good and dozing better and was discernibly less enlarged, so I was cheerful yet not very energized… In 3 days, I was down 2.75 pounds yet significantly all the more astonishing was that I increased a little over an a large portion of a pound of muscle. WOWSERS. I gauged myself again just no doubt and it was right. I'm composing this post with an immense smile all over and I feel stunning.

Another result of the arrangement is my stunning glucose control – I've had no lows or highs and am presently encountering the best numbers in months! I'm anticipating sharing every one of the plans I've made so far one week from now however here is the SIRT juice formula for the present.

SIRT juice

Serves: 1 juice

This makes enough for 1 juice, since you need 3 every day for the initial 3 days - I made enough for 2 days one after another. Less tidy up and all prepared a day ahead of time!

Fixings

2 bunches (75g) kale

Bunch (30g) rocket <- - this is British for arugula

5g parsley

150g green celery (2-3 stalks)

½ green apple

½ lemon - squeezed

½ level tsp of Matcha powder (green tea likewise has caffeine so just add to initial 2 juices of the day)

Guidelines

Juice fixings, ought to have 250ml (1 cup) when done - enough for 1 juice.

Include Matcha powder, shake or mix to consolidate and drink.

When was the last time you felt really well and looked awesome?

The New Year is flooded with craze diets that guarantee to change this yet only here and there convey benefits past an underlying weight loss prosper that dissipates like a phantom well before the primary green shoots of spring. With 99% of individuals setting out on diets neglecting to see enduring weight loss there truly is just a single sureness: trend diets don't work.

In any case, shouldn't something be said about a method for eating that conveys enormous outcomes for the time being, yet significantly greater outcomes in the long haul? Envision a framework reboot where you lose 7lbs in 7 days for an increasingly conditioned and lean you. Envision returning to sometime in the past to stir a profound feeling of imperativeness and having packs of vitality. Envision continually looking incredible and feeling genuinely well.

Did you realize that by eating certain nourishments – known as Sirtfoods – you can turn on your muscle to fat ratio's consuming forces, supercharge weight loss and fight off infection? Welcome to

The Sirtfood Diet – the progressive method to lose 7lb in 7 days and remain lean forever. Instances of Sirtfoods incorporate kale, rocket, pecans, additional virgin olive oil, dull chocolate, green tea and even espresso (indeed, espresso!). These are only a portion of the nourishments that have the ability to actuate sirtuins – our 'thin qualities' – which turns on a reusing procedure in our cells that makes us consume fat, form muscle and improve wellbeing.

If that sounds unrealistic, simply investigate the slimmest, most advantageous and longest lived societies on earth and you will see they share one thing in like manner: they all eat diets overflowing with Sirtfoods. Regardless of whether you look East to Okinawa, renowned for its record breaking number of centenarians, or West to the conventional Mediterranean diet, commended for its capacity to cut the danger of for all intents and purposes every constant malady, Sirtfoods are the regular connection.

It's no big surprise that it's become the must-do diet for competitors and superstars in 2016. Model and TV moderator Jodie Kidd says Sirtfoods are her "mystery to looking incredible" while title holder fighter David Haye credits Sirtfoods for helping him "accomplish a body creation and prosperity already unfathomable." Just envision what they could accomplish for you?

The best part is that The Sirtfood Diet is a diet of incorporation. No calorie checking, no barring entire nutrition classes, not in any event, staying away from the nourishments you love (chocolate, curry and espresso are all on the menu). It's tied in with appreciating what you put on your plate, not feeling sad about what you need to take off.

The Sirtfood Diet incorporates a set-by-step plan, with simple to follow plans, making it easy to receive these rewards. For those gunning to begin, why not attempt our authority Sirtfood green juice – the most advantageous green juice you will ever drink – to truly kick off your 2016 prosperity objectives.

Sirtfood Green Juice (serves 1)

Fixings:

2 huge bunches (75g) kale

a huge bunch (30g) rocket a little bunch (5g) level leaf parsley

a little bunch (5g) lovage leaves (discretionary)

2–3 enormous stalks (150g) green celery, including its leaves

1/2 medium green apple

juice of 1/2 lemon

1/2 level tsp matcha green tea

Guidelines:

Blend the greens (kale, rocket, parsley and lovage, if utilizing) together, then squeeze them. We discover juicers can truly differ in their effectiveness at squeezing verdant vegetables and you may need to re-squeeze the leftovers before proceeding onward to different fixings. The objective is to wind up with about 50ml of juice from the greens.

Presently squeeze the celery and apple.

You can strip the lemon and put it through the juicer too, yet we think that its a lot simpler to just crush the lemon by hand into the juice. By this stage, you ought to have around 250ml of juice altogether, maybe somewhat more.

It is just when the juice is made and prepared to serve that you include the matcha green tea. Pour a limited quantity of the juice into a glass, then include the matcha and mix vivaciously with a fork or teaspoon. We just use matcha in the initial two beverages of the day as it contains moderate measures of caffeine (a similar substance as a typical cup of tea). For individuals not accustomed to it, it might keep them alert if alcoholic late.

Once the matcha is broken down include the rest of the juice. Give it a last mix, then your juice is prepared to drink. Don't hesitate to top up with plain water, according to taste.

SIRTFOOD SMOOTHIE

Perhaps the best thing about being home is my mum's nourishment! Buzzword I know, yet we are so fortunate in light of the fact that we

LOVE to eat very similar things; solid, crisp, generally veggie lover, astonishing quality nourishment.

Preparing nourishment that we both love is such a delight and is exceptional quality time together that I acknowledge to such an extent. It's generally so much enjoyment as well, be that as it may, we are perfect young ladies, as is the kitchen a short time later, the two of us have an inclination toward OCD 'Howard Hughes' spotless 😄 (mum more than me obviously lol)

As a rule, the smoothies are my area however mum educated me concerning this and I needed to attempt it. I love to make smoothies that are basic, with as hardly any fixings as conceivable to support assimilation and not overpower our framework.

This one is the inverse, it senses that it has pretty much everything in it, however it tastes so great! Whats more, the fixings are for the most part Sirt nourishments. These nourishments have been appeared by research to turn on our 'thin gees' similarly as fasting and exercise does. In this way, in principle eating these nourishments is actually eating yourself thin! Too great not to attempt, what would i be able to state, it addressed that old diet insane in me!

This smoothie isn't for weak willed, the stew and turmeric sneak up all of a sudden, BUT, it is overflowing with supplements and you won't be ravenous after this I guarantee you! Check out this one, if you dare...

100g natural Greek or coconut yogurt

6 pecan parts

8-10 strawberries

Bunch of kale (stalks expelled)

1 tbsp crude cacao powder

1 pitted date (Medjool)

1 tsp turmeric

1-2mm cut of winged animals eye bean stew

200ml unsweetened almond milk

The diet vows to burn fat in seven days while leaving muscle immaculate. In any case, there's something else entirely to Sirtfoods than supernatural occurrence claims – if the science behind it looks at, it could develop that we've been considering smart dieting the incorrect path for a considerable length of time

You've known about the Sirt Diet somehow, regardless of whether you don't perceive the name. In news reports, it's displayed as the kilo-destroying plan that lets you eat chocolate and drink red wine, and vows to have resembling a supermodel and feeling like a superhuman.

On Instagram, it's the thing UFC featherweight champ Conor McGregor does – the Irishman took a selfie while finding out about it a couple of days before the first of his two major 2016 battles against Nate Diaz and scooped a better than expected 116,000 preferences.

To Cosmo perusers, it's what Jodie Kidd and Adele do – and, obviously, to naysayers it's simply the most recent prevailing fashion, another calorie-limitation and-juice trick that is making guarantees it can't in any way, shape or form keep.

In any case, the truth of the matter is, there's much more scientific clout behind Sirt than the normal drop-fat-quick arrangement. It depends on a class of exacerbates that have been found distinctly in the previous decade, and exploratory proof recommends that they're definitely more significant than recently suspected. What's more, if the individuals behind it are correct, we have to modify our center when we're thinking about what to eat.

Is the Sirt Diet Just Another Fad?

What's reality? What's the proof? Also, what's the science behind everything?

Initially, the science. Sirtuins – from which Sirt gets its name – are a gathering of Silent Information Regulator (SIR) proteins that increase our digestion, increment muscle proficiency, switch on fat-consuming procedures, diminish aggravation and fix harm in cells. In synopsis, sirtuins make us fitter, less fatty and more beneficial (there's additionally proof that they may help battle genuine infections, for example, Alzheimer's and diabetes – more on that later).

Gentle types of pressure – including activity and calorie limitation – trigger the body's creation of sirtuins, yet it's as of late been found that substance mixes known as sirtuin activators, found normally in products of the soil, can do something very similar. Certain nourishments – Sirtfoods, as they've been named by diet makers Aidan Goggins and Glen Matten – are particularly high in these sirtuin activators thus, the hypothesis goes, if you eat a diet generally made out of these nourishments you'll lose fat and improve your wellbeing.

To test this thought, Goggins and Matten made the Sirt Diet, the seven-day eating plan that is caused all the whine. It's straightforward enough: during the initial three days, day by day calorie admission is constrained to 1,000 and comprises of three green juices, in addition to a Sirtfood-rich supper. On days four to seven, calorie admission is expanded to 1,500 and comprises of two juices and two dinners. After that full scale first week, the proposal is to eat a reasonable diet rich in Sirtfoods, alongside increasingly green juices. On its substance, this sounds dreadful: even most fasting diets permit more calories. Be that as it may, is it?

"I didn't feel hard done by any means," says Rannoch Donald, a mentor and mentor who attempted the diet. "The juice is critical: it resembles rocket fuel. After the underlying week, following the diet was plain cruising, and following three weeks I was 5kg lighter.

However, critically, I additionally felt the best I have in two or three years. I lost muscle versus fat, I was dozing better, I had no gut issues, I was feeling invigorated... I was instructing and preparing about six classes every week with incredible recuperation, even from the most tiring Brazilian jiu jitsu session."

To test the diet on a more extensive scale, Goggins and Matten enlisted 37 individuals from KX Gym in London, 15 of whom were overweight. All had been doing a moderate measure of activity; none expanded it and some even started doing less. Furthermore, the outcomes in only multi week, in any event, thinking about the calorie limitation, were bewildering: the guineas pigs lost a normal of 3kg of fat yet put on around 0.8kg of muscle. With a standard diet that cut calories by a similar sum in seven days, you'd hope to lose a limit of 1kg.

For what reason are there no Sirt supps?

It's the conspicuous inquiry: if sirtuins are so game-changing, for what reason aren't pharmaceutical and supplement organizations scrambling to distil them into pill structure? Short answer: on the grounds that the component by which they work despite everything isn't completely comprehended, implying that supps won't really be also consumed by the body as the regular structures.

Goggins and Matten point to the case of resveratrol. "In supplement structure it's ineffectively consumed by the body, yet in its common nourishment grid of red wine, its bioavailability (how much the body can utilize) is in any event sixfold higher. We trust it's smarter to expend a wide scope of these supplements as regular wholefoods, where they exist together nearby the many other characteristic bioactive plant synthetics which act synergistically to help our wellbeing." at the end of the day: eat better, instead of simply popping a pill.

Quick and enraged?

Obviously, this is the part of the Sirt Diet that has pundits wailing. Most point to the way that, in any event in the underlying stages, the arrangement centers around calorie limitation and that, according to past understanding, weight loss over 1kg seven days is undesirable or impractical. It's a substantial worry: in most calorie-limitation diets, early weight loss will in general originate from calorie consumption and diminished water-swelling, and – as ongoing examination on candidates in TV's The Biggest Loser appears – essentially proportioning yourself consistently can ease back your digestion to a close lasting creep, just as disturbing your body's degrees of "hunger hormone" ghrelin, making you for all time hungry.

In any case, Goggins and Matten counter, this isn't what Sirt does. Indeed, the diet impersonates a few parts of fasting, and in the initial seven days of the full diet Sirtfoods appear to turbo-charge the impacts of calorie limitation. Be that as it may, it's more entangled than simply starving yourself for momentary changes. So how can it work? All things considered, right off the bat, it's fundamental to comprehend the "stress" some portion of the condition. "Everybody needs some measure of worry in their lives," says Goggins. "Each time we train we make a weight on the body, which can be something worth being thankful for or an awful thing. There's an impulse to consistently prepare more earnestly, to invest more energy, however that conveys a danger of working up constant pressure, which conveys the danger of burnout and a debilitated invulnerable framework."

The flipside: by presenting your body to poor quality wellsprings of stress, you'll increment your body's capacity to adapt. "Plant pressure reactions are in reality more advanced than our own," clarifies Goggins. "Consider it: if we are eager and parched we can go looking for nourishment and drink; excessively hot – we discover conceal; enduring an onslaught – we can escape. Interestingly, plants are stationary and must persevere through every one of the boundaries of these physiological burdens and dangers. In result, in the course of recent years they have built up an exceptionally complex pressure reaction framework that lowers [humans'] by creating an immense assortment of characteristic plant synthetic concoctions – called polyphenols – that permit them to effectively adjust to their condition and endure. When we devour these plants, we additionally expend these polyphenol supplements, which actuate our very own inborn pressure reaction pathways. We're speaking here about the very same pathways that fasting and exercise switch on – the sirtuins."

Polyphenols, according to Goggins, are the one thing the normal American diet has enough of, and when deprived of them the much-praised Mediterranean diet loses practically the entirety of its viability. By means of Sirtfoods, polyphenols have a large group of weight-the executives impacts, including empowering white fat tissue (customarily the terrible stuff) to emulate darker fat tissue (the "great" fat that assists with creating body heat). They likewise help totality issues, by improving your body's affectability to the satiety hormone leptin.

"These common plant mixes are currently alluded to as 'calorie limitation mimetics' because of their capacity to turn on indistinguishable positive changes in our phones from would be seen during fasting, for example, fat consuming," says Goggins. "The suggestions are down evolving. When we're furnished with further developed flagging mixes than we produce ourselves, the results are better than anything we can accomplish alone."

The genuine wellbeing nourishments

There's likewise more to Sirt than body piece. Outside Goggins and Matten's tests, all the more scientifically controlled preliminaries on single Sirtfoods have demonstrated promising outcomes. In October 2015, for example, scientists at Columbia University in New York found that drinking water with a gram of cocoa – particularly rich in the sirtuin activator epicatechin – broke up in it prompted improved memory in 19 moderately aged subjects.

In November that year, specialists at Monash University in Melbourne revealed that when patients in the beginning times of type 2 diabetes included a gram of turmeric daily to their diets, it improved their working memory. For diabetics, there's some proof that sirtuin enactment builds the measure of insulin that can be emitted and causes it work all the more adequately. In the skeleton, sirtuins advance the creation and endurance of osteoblasts, a kind of cell answerable for building new bone.

The following huge thing for Sirt, when more research is performed, will be in its relationship to leucine, the principle muscle-developer among the expanded chain amino acids (BCAAs). Leucine is a key controller of protein combination and initiates a protein known as mTOR (in spite of the fact that you don't have to stress over that to comprehend the following piece).

"Leucine is a twofold edged sword," clarifies Goggins. "It's a quickening agent for muscle development, however if you don't have the interior hardware to manage it, the motor detonates." In principle, having a more Sirtfood-substantial diet could expand the measure of protein your body can effectively absorb, transferring the old "20-30g a sitting" proposal solidly to the past.

Obviously, the entirety of this needs more research. Thirty-seven individuals in a single rec center isn't a lot of an example size, and different investigations on the impacts of sirtuins have been done on creatures or human cells – neither ensured to precisely think about what goes inside the body. In any case, for all the analysis of the diet's increasingly extreme cases, it's difficult to perceive what you remain to lose by following some rendition of the Sirt Diet. Regardless of whether you set aside the calorie-limited adaptation of the arrangement and hop directly to "upkeep" mode, you'd eat an immense assortment of the nourishments identified as key in the alleged Blue Zones, territories of the world like Sardinia and Okinawa where individuals live more, more beneficial lives.

"I don't care for the word diet, yet this is diet as in lifestyle instead of some handy solution mediation," says Donald. "It's basically about eating great. Furthermore, in spite of the presence of green juice drinks, the general way of thinking is about the incorporation of solid entire common fixings as opposed to the deification of 'superfoods'." Or, to put it another way: you're probably not going to get less sound by getting more kale, berries, pecans and red wine into your diet. Regardless of whether you aren't a supermodel or a UFC warrior.

Sirtfood Diet Essentials

These are the most elevated appraised 20 nourishments for a Sirtfood-rich diet, and how you can fuse them into your day by day dinners

10,000 foot bean stew Also sold as Thai chillies, they're more strong than normal bean stews, and furthermore progressively pressed with supplements. Use them to set off sweet or harsh plans.

Buckwheat Technically a pseudo-grain: it's really a natural product seed identified with rhubarb. Additionally accessible in noodle structure (as soba), however ensure you're getting the without wheat adaptation.

ades on the off chance that you're pondering, they're salted blossom buds. Sprinkle them over plate of mixed greens or cooked cauliflower.

Celery The hearts and leaves are the most nutritious part, so don't discard them if you're mixing up a shake.

Cocoa The flavonol-rich kind improves circulatory strain, glucose control and cholesterol. Search for a high level of cacao.

Espresso Drink it dark – some proof milk can diminish the assimilation of sirtuin-initiating supplements.

Additional virgin olive oil The additional virgin kind has more Sirt benefits, and an all the more fulfilling, peppery taste.

Green tea or matcha Add a cut of lemon to build retention of sirtuin-delivering supplements. Matcha is far better, however go Japanese, not Chinese, to maintain a strategic distance from potential lead pollution.

Kale Includes tremendous measures of sirtuin-actuating supplements quercetin and kaempferol. Back rub it with olive oil and lemon juice to serve it as a plate of mixed greens.

Lovage It's a herb. Become your very own on a windowsill, and toss it into sautés.

Medjool dates They're a powerful 66% sugar, yet - with some restraint - don't raise glucose levels, and have really been connected to brought down paces of diabetes and coronary illness.

Parsley More than only an enhancement – it's high in apigenin. Toss it into a smoothie or juice for the full advantage.

Chicory Red is ideal, however yellow works fine. Toss it in a plate of mixed greens.

Red onion The red assortment's better for you, and sufficiently sweet to eat crude. Cleave it and add to a serving of mixed greens, or eat it with a burger.

Red wine You've known about resveratrol: the uplifting news is, it's warmth stable, so you can get profits by cooking with it (just as glugging it straight). Pinot noir has the most noteworthy substance.

Rocket One of the least meddled with plate of mixed greens accessible. Shower it with olive oil.

Soy Soybeans and miso are high in sirtuin activators. Remember it for sautés.

Strawberries Though they're sweet, they just contain 1tsp of sugar per 100g – and look into proposes they improve your body's capacity to deal with sugary carbs.

Turmeric Evidence recommends the curcumin in it has hostile to disease properities. It's difficult for the body to acclimatize alone, however cooking it in fluid and including fat and dark pepper expands assimilation.

in fat and calories, yet settled in lessening metabolic
sh them up with parsley for sirt-enhanced pesto.

Each diet plan has a thought behind it. Sirtfood diet depends on the idea of nourishments which help to enact a class of proteins called sirtuins, a protein type to a great extent associated with cell guideline, maturing and digestion of the body. According to an examination, sirtuins additionally causes the body to support its component and consume fats and decrease irritation and lower cholesterol levels.

Nourishments Included In Sirtfood Diet

Red wine

Dull chocolate

Parsley

Citrus natural products

Green tea

Berries like strawberries and blueberries

Red onion

Turmeric

Apples

Kale

Soy

Pecans

Buckwheat

10,000 foot chillies

Virgin olive oil

lovage

Red chicory

Sirtfood Diet Plan

The sirtfood diet plan is separated into two simple stages. In the main stage, you need to confine your calorie admission to 1000 cal/day for the initial three days which will incorporate three sirtfood green juices and a one-time dinner loaded up with sirtfoods. In the initial three days, an individual may feel hungry however from the fourth to the seventh day, the starvation may somewhat go down as the individual may build the calorie admission from 1000 to 1500 cal/day. This will incorporate two sirtfood green juices and two dinners every day. To get ready green juices, individuals may select from celery, kale, green tea and parsley while for dinners, chicken, kale curry, prawns fry, turkey and buckwheat will be the best choices.

The second period of sirtfood is really when weight loss begins to occur. This stage takes 14 days in which an individual expends three sirtfood-rich suppers every day alongside an exceptional green juice.

This assists with shedding seven pounds in seven days. Both the periods of the diet are planned on the plan to eat the sound and nutritive nourishments what nature offers.

How Can It Work?

The primary guideline behind sirtfood diet is that it enacts the fat-decreasing procedure in the body alongside advancing bulk development. Be that as it may, the inquiry that emerges in everybody's psyche in the wake of realizing the initial two stages is what really occurs after the third seven day stretch of the diet?

Indeed, the possibility of sirtfood diet is that it is for the individuals who truly cherished the initial two periods of the diet and need to proceed on a smart dieting way. Sirtfood diet isn't just about dieting for those three weeks yet picking this diet plan as a lifestyle. This diet plan is so successful and solid that individuals who have seen the outcomes will definitely be urged to keep drinking green squeezes each day and incorporate sirtfood in their suppers. Regardless of whether, holding fast to this diet plan is unimaginable consistently, simply having sound nourishment and including a touch of sirtfood the top will do extraordinary advantage to your body.

According to a pilot study directed by Aidan and Glen, a specialist in healthful medication drug store, it is demonstrated that individuals have lost around 7 lbs in 7 days with no lessening in their bulk. Those individuals have likewise revealed an expansion in their vitality, better rest and improvement of their skin.

Any diet that lets you eat chocolate, wine and espresso will undoubtedly draw intrigue. Be that as it may, can you truly get more fit and remain sound on the Sirtfood Diet? The artist Adele supposedly utilized it to thin down. Be that as it may, nourishment specialists state the new diet prevailing fashion has advantages and disadvantages.

"The Sirtfood Diet" book was distributed in January by Aidan Goggins and Glen Matten, alumni of the University of Surrey in England who both have graduate degrees in dietary prescription. It advances a mix of calorie limitation, green juices and suppers stuffed with sirtuins.

What the hell are sirtuins? Dissimilar to carbs, fats and proteins, we don't hear this sustenance term bandied about in other diet books and wellbeing magazines commonly.

"They're a piece of a group of proteins. Concentrates in creatures show they help control cell capacities - things like digestion. They're extremely uncommon. Creature examines are demonstrating they can help with life span and maturing," Erin Morse, boss clinical dietitian at UCLA Health, disclosed to CBS News.

A large number of the sirtuin-rich nourishments advanced in the diet are plant-based, including blueberries, strawberries, kale, arugula (called rocket in the U.K.), chocolate (as long as it's 85 percent genuine cocoa), citrus, espresso and matcha green tea.

Be that as it may, the huge proviso, Morse stated, is the creature study part. No human investigations have demonstrated the advantages of eating nourishments rich in sirtuins.

"The issue with this diet is that there aren't human examinations - long haul or huge," she clarified. "This is unquestionably new and look into is positively rising on this subject."

Marion Nestle, educator of sustenance, nourishment studies and general wellbeing at New York University, was doubtful about the advantages of surtuins.

"Sirtuins are chemicals and, therefore, proteins. Most proteins don't endure stomach corrosive or protein-processing compounds in the small digestive tract so the likelihood of their endurance isn't incredible," she disclosed to CBS News.

The Sirtfood Diet packs in nourishments high in sirtuins, including green juices produced using kale, celery, arugula, parsley, green tea and lemon.

For the initial three days of the diet, you're limited to three of those green juices in addition to one sirtfood-based feast a day, totaling close to 1,000 calories for every day.

On the fourth through the seventh days, 1,500 calories daily are permitted, including two sirtuin-filled juices and two dinners.

A 14-day support stage then follows and dieters can swallow a green juice in addition to three sirtfood dinners daily.

Both Morse and Nestle said the early calorie limitation stage is the genuine mystery to the diet's weight-loss guarantees.

"They must child. Anybody would get in shape - and bunches of it - on 1,500 calories every day, with or without sirtuins," Nestle said.

She said it's essentially a starvation diet, which can cause bulk loss and lack of hydration.

"Luckily, the body battles starvation so the vast majority can't adhere to low-calorie diets for long, and half a month on this diet shouldn't make any difference much," Nestle said.

Morse said the underlying weight loss dieters may encounter won't probably be fat loss, yet rather a shedding of water weight.

"The vast majority won't see a fat loss in those early days. Likely it's water. You'll feel slimmer, yet it's presumably water weight. You can't lose fat in that short a measure of time," Morse clarified.

"For a modest lady who is 5 feet tall and not exceptionally dynamic, it's not risky, yet 1,000 calories would be excessively low for a 6-foot-4-inch man to devour," said Morse.

Anybody with an interminable condition, for example, diabetes, where sugar levels are critical to follow, could confront progressively genuine wellbeing dangers, she included.

On the in addition to side, you can't turn out badly with a diet loaded with vegetables and foods grown from the ground fats, (for example, those found in nuts and olive oil), Morse said.

"Rocket and parsley and celery and green apples - those are on the whole great things. Furthermore, green tea - matcha - has calming properties. There are human examinations with green tea. Pecans are high in sound fats, fiber and protein," Morse said.

An investigation out this week in JAMA Internal Medicine backs up the benefit of stacking up on plant-based proteins. Massachusetts General Hospital and Harvard Medical School scientists considered the diets of in excess of 130,000 individuals and found that eating more protein from plant sources was connected with a lower danger of death. Expending more protein from creature sources was related with a higher danger of death, particularly among grown-ups who had at least one unfortunate propensities, for example, smoking, drinking or being inactive.

The Sirtfood Diet additionally requires heaps of nourishment arranging and planning time, and Morse said individuals who plan their suppers ahead of time normally have more weight-loss achievement.

"I would prescribe parts of this diet, however I for one wouldn't suggest this diet. I surmise I don't care for the term 'diet.' There's such a great amount of disappointment with diet. You're instructed sure transient objectives and how to eat a specific way and afterward individuals will in general go off and restore more weight," Morse stated, taking note of that she lean towards a general lifestyle-based arrangement that individuals can adhere to forever.

The early "starvation" period of the diet aside, Nestle additionally said the plant-substantial eating plan has plusses.

"The nourishments that are proposed in this diet are brilliant decisions," she said. "If it encourages individuals who need to get in shape to lose a few, I'm for it."

LOSE 7LBS IN 7 DAYS

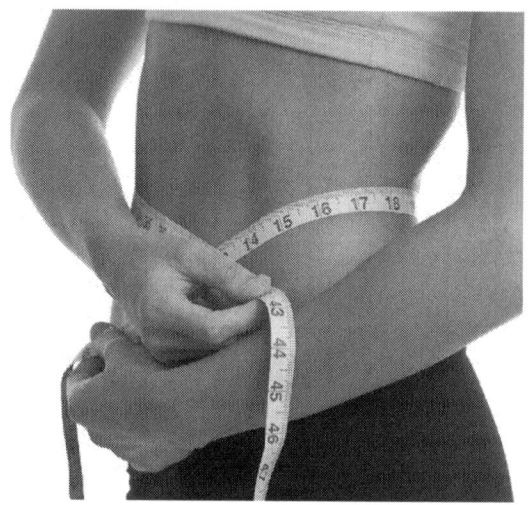

The Sirtfood Diet is the weight loss plan everybody's discussing – not least since it permits you to appreciate things most systems boycott, including chocolate, red wine and espresso.

Here, in a -exclusive concentrate from their new book, The Sirtfood Diet nutritionists and writers Aidan Goggins and Glen Matten clarify why each chomp of their diet will carry you closer to the thin body you've constantly longed for.

Being specialists in healthful prescription, it is reasonable for state that dieting has never been our thing.

That all changed when we found sirtfoods – nourishments that support weight loss and lift your wellbeing all the while.

Presently we've taken the most powerful sirtfoods on earth and woven them into a spic and span diet – a festival of nourishment that makes you need to get a knife and fork, not lay them down.

Our arrangement has been supported by top competitors including fighter David Haye , Olympic mariner Sir Ben Ainslie and rugby player James Haskell.

Television gourmet expert Lorraine Pascale depicted it as "a non-faddy diet that offers amazing medical advantages and weight loss," while moderator Jodie Kidd said she felt "relentless" on the diet.

The science bit: Why sirtfoods are extraordinary

Sirtfoods are an as of late found gathering of ordinary plant nourishments, known as sirtuin activators, which switch on our 'thin' qualities – similar qualities enacted by exercise and fasting.

Alongside this fat-consuming impact, sirtfoods likewise have the extraordinary capacity to -naturally control hunger and increment muscle work – making them the ideal answer for accomplishing a sound weight.

In fact, their wellbeing boosting impacts are ground-breaking to such an extent that a few examinations have demonstrated them to be more powerful than physician endorsed sedates in forestalling constant illness, with clear -benefits in diabetes, coronary illness and -Alzheimer's ailment.

No big surprise societies eating the most sirtfoods – including Japan and Italy – are the least fatty and most advantageous on the planet. Also, that is the reason we've contrived a diet based around them.

THE SIRTFOOD LIST

Sirtfoods are generally promptly accessible and -accessible nourishments. The most strong ones include: red wine, dull chocolate, dark espresso, kale, rocket, parsley, red onions, strawberries, pecans, additional virgin olive oil, curry flavors, green tea, blueberries, celery, bean stew, apples and buckwheat.

What's the proof?

We trialed our diet at a rec center in South West London, fundamentally to test and improve wellbeing. We were paralyzed by the outcomes. Members regularly lost 7lbs in seven days, and saw increments in bulk, prosperity and vitality.

We anticipated that individuals should lose some weight yet never foreseen that it would be so a lot, nor that individuals would keep up or even increase some muscle, which is strange when dieting.

Beginning

The one bit of unit you have to follow the Sirtfood Diet is a juicer to make the fundamental day by day green juices. While there's bunches of discussion about which juicers are ideal, we're not very hung up on that. Simply get one that you can bear.

You'll likewise need to get some matcha green tea powder to add to your juices as it's an intense fat-consuming sirtfood. Attempt Love Matcha Grade Green Tea Powder (£6.99 for 50g, from Amazon). Another option – in spite of the fact that not as ground-breaking – is to let the powder alone for the juice and drink three cups of green tea day by day.

Your supper organizer

This diet depends on a two phase, three-week plan. Week one is an escalated seven-day program intended to launch weight loss.

Weeks two and three are an upkeep plan intended for proceeded with weight loss (expect around 1-2lbs per week) and better wellbeing.

Pick your supper decisions from the rundown underneath.

WEEK 1

Day 1 to 3 (1,000 calories for every day)

Breakfast: Sirtfood green juice

Early in the day: Green juice

Lunch: Green juice

Supper: Choice from underneath, in addition to 15–20g dull chocolate

Day 4 to 7 (1,500 calories for each day)

Plan as above, yet you drop one of the day by day green squeezes and supplant it with a second day by day dinner – either a morning meal or lunch from the rundown underneath.

WEEKS 2 AND 3 (not calorie checked)

Every day ought to include:

3 x sirtfood fundamental dinners

1 sirtfood green juice

2 bites, look over a little bunch of pecans, strawberries or blueberries or an apple

Morning meals

Green juice (see formula underneath)

Sirtfood omelet – with bacon, parsley, chicory

Greek yogurt – with 10g ground dull chocolate, slashed pecans and blended berries

Spiced fried eggs – with stew and tumeric

Snacks

Prepared cod with sautéed greens

Vegetable and kidney bean stew with prepared potato

Potato plate of mixed greens with red onion, celery, apples and pecans

Prepared chicken bosom with pecan and parsley pesto and red onion plate of mixed greens

Suppers

Prawn pan sear with buckwheat noodles (see formula underneath)

Chicken bosom with tomato and bean stew salsa

Salmon filet with chicory, rocket and celery plate of mixed greens

Meat with red wine, onion rings and herb simmered potatoes (see formula beneath)

Tuscan bean stew (see formula underneath)

Sirtfood green juice (Serves 1)

2 huge bunches (75g) kale

Huge bunch (30g) rocket

Small bunch (5g) level leaf parsley

2–3 huge stalks (150g) green celery – including leaves

A large portion of a green apple

Juice of half lemon and half tsp matcha.

To make:

Squeeze every one of the fixings aside from the green tea. Then blend a modest quantity of juice in a glass with the matcha and mix overwhelmingly with a fork, then include the remainder of the juice to the glass and blend once more.

You can make up the entirety of your juices for the day in one clump toward the beginning of the day, and refrigerate until required.

Prawn Stir-fry with Noodles (serves 1)

Prawn pan sear with noodles

Solid: Prawn pan sear with noodles

150g shelled crude prawns

2 tsp soy sauce

2 tsp additional virgin olive oil

75g soba (buckwheat noodles)

1 hacked garlic clove

1 hacked superior stew

1 tsp finely hacked crisp ginger

20g red onions - cut

40g celery, cut,

75g green beans - hacked,

50g hacked kale,

100ml chicken stock.

To make:

Cook the prawns in a hot skillet with 1tsp of the soy and 1 tsp of the oil for 2 minutes and put to the other side. Cook the noodles as coordinated on the parcel. Channel and put in a safe spot.

In the interim, fry flavors and veg in the rest of the oil over a medium–high warmth for 2–3 minutes. Add the stock and bring to the bubble, then stew for a moment or two, until the vegetables are cooked yet at the same time crunchy.

Add the prawns and noodles to the skillet, take back to the bubble. Expel from the warmth and serve.

Hamburger with red wine, onion rings and herb broiled potatoes

Hamburger with red wine, onion rings and herb-broiled potatoes

Generous: Beef with red wine, onion rings and herb-broiled potatoes

100g potatoes - stripped and cut into 2cm lumps

1 tbsp additional virgin olive oil

5g parsley - finely slashed

50g red onion-cut into rings

50g cut kale

1 garlic clove - finely slashed

150g hamburger steak

40ml red wine

150ml hamburger stock

1 tsp tomato purée

1 tsp cornflour - broke down in 1 tbsp water

To make:

Warmth the stove to 220C/gas 7. Heat up the potatoes for 5 minutes, then channel. Spot in a simmering tin with 1 tsp of the oil and dish for 35–45 minutes. Turn like clockwork. When cooked, expel, sprinkle with the cleaved parsley and blend well.

Fry onion in 1 tsp of the oil over a medium warmth for 5–7 minutes, until pleasantly caramelized. Steam the kale for 2–3 minutes then channel. Fry the garlic delicately in 1/2 teaspoon of oil for 1 moment, until delicate, include the kale and fry for a further 1–2 minutes, until delicate.

Coat the hamburger with 1/2 a teaspoon of the oil and fry in a hot skillet over a medium warmth, according to how you like it cooked. Expel from the dish and put aside to rest.

Add the wine to the hot dish and diminish considerably, until syrupy. Include the stock and tomato purée and bring to the bubble, then add the cornflour glue to thicken, a little at once. Serve meat with cook potatoes, kale, onion rings and red wine sauce.

Tuscan bean stew (Serves 1)

1 tbsp additional virgin olive oil

50g red onion, finely hacked 30g carrot, finely cleaved 30g celery, finely slashed

1 garlic clove, finely hacked

1 tsp herbes de Provence 200ml vegetable stock

1 x 400g tin hacked tomatoes 1 tsp tomato purée

200g tinned blended beans

50g kale, hacked

1 tbsp hacked parsley

40g buckwheat to serve

To make:

Warmth oil in a pot over a low–medium warmth and tenderly fry the onion, carrot, celery, garlic and herbs, until the veg are delicate.

Include the stock, tomatoes and tomato purée and bring to the bubble. Include the beans and stew for 30 minutes. Include the kale and cook for another 5–10 minutes, until delicate, then include the parsley.

Cook the buckwheat according to bundle directions, channel and serve.

Continuously check with your primary care physician before beginning any new diet.

Just the diet of 2016 – and you'll be satisfied to realize that not at all like numerous prevailing fashions, there's science to back it up.

It centers around the utilization of sirtfoods, which have been found to have a similar impact on the body as 5:2, yet without the muscle loss or peevishness brought about by being restricted to 500 calories per day.

Sirtfoods are a newfound gathering of nourishments pressed with supplements that have a similar impact as fasting (for example fat consuming is invigorated and the our restoring cells are turned on).

So as opposed to limiting yourself, you could be tucking into Pinot Noir or 85 percent cocoa chocolate and as yet getting more fit.

The rundown of sirtfoods is broad, and just as the feature getting red wine and chocolate, incorporates buckwheat, celery, stew, espresso, additional virgin olive oil, matcha tea, kale, medjool dates, parsley, red onion, rocket, soy, strawberries, turmeric and pecans.

Curiously, nations where they as of now expend huge measure of these nourishments, for example, Japan and Italy, are positioned as probably the most advantageous on the planet.

Who thought of the Sirtfood Diet?

The creators of The Sirtfood Diet, Aidan Goggins and Glen Matten, are qualified in healthful medication, and shockingly, never set out to dispatch a weight-loss program.

Be that as it may, a year ago they led a pilot preliminary after the disclosure that sirtuins, the quality in the body enacted by sirtfoods, could impact our vulnerability to illness.

Goggins and Matten put 40 individuals on another sirtfood-rich system, and immediately found that the advantages were not simply wellbeing boosting as envisioned – the analyzers were likewise losing by and large a large portion of a stone in seven days.

How can it work?

The diet Goggins and Matten thought of includes two stages.

The principal keeps going seven days – with days one to three comprising of three sirtfood-rich green juices, in addition to one full sirtfood-stuffed feast a day, limiting every day calorie admission to 1000 (still twice as much as 5:2).

Days four to seven incorporate two juices and two suppers, taking you up to 1500 calories.

Stage two is the upkeep stage, and keeps going 14 days.

Every day you have three adjusted sirtfood-rich dinners, one green juice and two or three discretionary tidbits. Look at the current month's Good Housekeeping magazine for all the juice and dinner plans.

For what reason is it superior to different diets?

During their pilot study, Goggins and Matten said numerous members detailing that the segment sizes were too huge – proposing that just as topping you off, sirtfoods likewise smother your hunger.

Another difference that separates this from, for instance, 5:2, is that in the preliminary, 64 percent of analyzers either kept up or expanded their bulk, staying away from the feared withered look that is often connected with quick weight loss.

Goodness, and did we notice you can at present eat chocolate?!

Who's tailing it?

After it began in a swanky West London rec center, The Sirtfood Diet has picked up ubiquity, and big names including model/moderators Lorraine Pascale and Jodie Kidd, heavyweight fighter David Haye and gold-medla winning mariner Ben Ainslie all depend on it.

A serious solid looking bundle, if ever we saw one!

Our Deputy Editor, Michelle Hather, has additionally tried The Sirtfood Diet. Here's her decision:

'If you are searching for a diet that turbo charges your weight loss then this is an incredible one. That first week is very entangled yet the nourishment was totally heavenly – my most loved was the veg bean stew that had a concealed element of cocoa! Any diet must be a lifestyle as opposed to a prevailing fashion and, if you can find a good pace the squeezing and you like cooking without any preparation, I think this is a champ.'

WHITE BEAN AND TUNA SALAD WITH BASIL VINAIGRETTE

Fixings:

Legitimate salt and pepper

12 oz. green beans, cut and split

1 little shallot, hacked

1 c. daintily stuffed basil leaves

3 tbsp. olive oil

1 tbsp. red wine vinegar

4 c. torn lettuce

1 15-oz would small be able to white beans, washed

2 5-oz jars strong white fish in water, depleted

4 delicate bubbled eggs, divided

Headings:

Heat an enormous pot of water to the point of boiling. Include 1 tablespoon salt, then green beans, and cook until simply delicate, 3 to 4 minutes. Channel and flush under virus water to cool.

In the meantime, in a blender, puree shallot, basil, oil, vinegar, and 1/2 teaspoon each salt and pepper until smooth.

Move half of dressing to huge bowl and hurl with green beans. Crease in lettuce, white beans, and fish and present with outstanding dressing and eggs.

Per serving: 340 calories, 16.5 g fat (3 g immersed), 31 g protein, 770 mg sodium, 24 g carb, 8 g fiber

RHUBARB AND CITRUS SALAD WITH BLACK PEPPER VINAIGRETTE

Fixings:

2 tbsp. nectar

2 tbsp. white wine vinegar

3 stalks rhubarb, cut and cut into 1-in. pieces

1/4 c. olive oil

Fit salt and pepper

2 Cara oranges

3 oz. infant spinach (around 4 c.)

2 bundles watercress, thick stems expelled

1/4 c. toasted pistachios, slashed

1 oz. ricotta salata, shaved

Headings:

In little bowl, whisk together nectar and vinegar. Add rhubarb and hurl to cover. Let remain at any rate 5 minutes and as long as 10 minutes, then include olive oil, 1/2 teaspoons salt and 2 teaspoons coarsely ground pepper.

In the meantime, remove strip and white substance from oranges, then meagerly cut.

In enormous bowl, hurl spinach and watercress; overlay in orange cuts and separation among plates. Spoon rhubarb and dressing over every serving of mixed greens and top with pistachios and ricotta salata.

Per serving: 280 calories, 19.5 g fat (3.5 g soaked), 5 g protein, 380 mg sodium, 25 g starch, 4 g fiber

Fixings:

Bundle of vegetable pot stickers or pierogies

2 tbsp. hoisin sauce

2 tbsp. new lime juice

1 tbsp. water

1 tbsp. vegetable oil

1 red pepper, daintily cut

1 yellow pepper, daintily cut

1 tbsp. finely hacked new ginger

1 little red onion, daintily cut

8 oz. snow peas, split corner to corner

Bearings:

Sauté vegetable pot stickers or pierogies in huge skillet per bundle headings; move to plate. Whisk together hoisin sauce, new lime squeeze, and water.

Add vegetable oil to skillet and warmth on medium. Include red pepper, yellow pepper, and finely cleaved crisp ginger and cook, hurling much of the time, 5 minutes. Include little red onion and cook, hurling, 1 moment.

Include snow peas and cook, secured, hurling often, until vegetables are simply delicate, around 4 minutes. Hurl vegetables with sauce and present with pot stickers.

Per serving: 240 calories, 6.5 g fat (0.5 g immersed fat), 7 g protein, 510 mg sodium, 41 g carb, 5 g fiber

CONCLUSION

If the abrupt ascent of one more popular expression has your head turning, permit us to separate it a bit. Sirt nourishments are so named in light of the fact that they contain sirtuins; a class of proteins which contain compounds that manage different pathways in the body. Up until now, so muddled. The part that interests sound eaters and dieters is that these proteins seem to confine calories, or impact our digestion, a reaction of which is known to slow maturing in numerous species. The Sirtfood Diet by Aiden Goggins and Glen Matten is the most recent tome setting individuals buzzing. A preliminary of the diet among exercise center goers demonstrated fast weight loss, yet the book centers for the most part around smart dieting — which we at HelloFresh love!

Discussion despite everything exists in the scientific network concerning whether this watched impact will work the equivalent precisely inside the human body. By and by, as a manual for considering the advantages entire nourishment can give us, we figure we'll give sirt nourishments the old school attempt. Moreover, we're as of now eating heaps of it!

Manufactured by Amazon.ca
Bolton, ON

12640480R00085